Islam

A Concise Introduction

Javed Ahmed Ghamidi

**Ghamidi Center
of Islamic Learning**

www.ghamidi.org   AN INITIATIVE OF AL-MAWRID US.

Ghamidi Center
of Islamic Learning
www.ghamidi.org   AN INITIATIVE OF AL-MAWRID US.

Publisher: Ghamidi Center of Islamic Learning - Al-Mawrid US
ISBN: 978-1-966600-34-3

Address: 3620 N Josey Ln, Suite 230 Carrollton, TX 75007
Website: www.ghamidi.org
Email: info@ghamidi.org

CONTENTS

Our Approach to Bringing Academic Works to a Global Audience

This book has been translated by the GCIL / Al-Mawrid US Translations Team, utilizing a state-of-the-art Artificial Intelligence (AI) system to ensure initial accuracy, fluency, and consistency. After the AI translation phase, the text undergoes a thorough multi-step human review to refine linguistic precision, cultural authenticity, and fidelity to the author's original intent.

Our review team—fluent in both the source and target languages—carefully proofreads, edits, and validates each section of the text. Special attention is given to technical expressions, academic references, and subtle nuances that automated systems may not fully capture. This process ensures that the author's meaning is conveyed to a Western, English-speaking audience with clarity, integrity, and in a familiar, natural style of English.

While every effort has been made to ensure accuracy and clarity, this work remains a human endeavor and may contain occasional errors or oversights. We welcome your feedback and suggestions for improvement at info@ghamidi.org

Contributors

Project Supervision: Farhan Saiyed
AI Translation: Muhammad Umair Ajmal
Initial Review: Danish Hamid
Detailed Review: Farhan Saiyed & Sohail Siddiqui
Layout Supervision: Muhammad Irtaza Ajmal
Typesetting & Layout: Tallal Bin Nasir
Cover Design: Muhammad Irtaza Ajmal & Hammad Khalid

PREFACE

In God's sight, the only true religion is Islam. I have explained my understanding of this religion in my book *Meezān*. This is a summary of that book, presenting the core subject matter in a simplified manner, separating it from its scholarly discussions and argumentations.

The understanding and interpretation of religion I have written and spoken about until now is the result of the mentorship of Ustadh Imām Amin Ahsan Islahi. Therefore, like all other books, this book is also dedicated to him:

طبع تو داد سر خط مشق سخن را
گوئی برات نور ز خاور گرفته ایم

Your nature unveiled the art of speech so fair,
You said, "I acquired it from the East's bright glare."

Javed Ahmed Ghamidi
Al-Mawrid, Lahore
25 December 2007

In the name of God, the Most Gracious,
the Eternally Compassionate

THE TRUE RELIGION

Religion is the guidance of God Almighty, first inspired in human nature and then provided to humanity through His Prophets, along with all necessary details. The final Prophet in this chain is Muhammad (PBUH)[1]. Hence, the sole source of religion now is his noble person, and the true religion is that which he declared to be religion through his words, actions, and both tacit[2] and explicit approvals. This religion has been transmitted to us through the consensus[3] of his companions and an unbroken chain of continuous verbal and practical transmission[4], preserved in two authentic forms:

1. Qur'ān
2. Sunna

---

1. Peace be upon him
2. This means that something appeared before the Prophet (PBUH) in the capacity of religion, and he did not forbid it.
3. That is, with complete agreement and without any disagreement.
4. That is, continuously and without interruption—reciting, writing, narrating, and practicing it from generation to generation.

1. Qur'ān

The Qur'ān is the book revealed by God Almighty to His final messenger, Muhammad (PBUH). Since its revelation, it has been faithfully preserved by the Muslim community, who firmly believe it remains exactly as it was revealed. The Prophet's (PBUH) companions were unanimous in affirming the integrity of its content and transmitted it to the world with exceptional care through their consensus and an unbroken chain of oral transmission without the slightest alteration.

2. Sunna

Sunna is the tradition of the Abrahamic religion, which the Prophet (PBUH) renewed, reformed, and with certain additions, implemented among his followers as religion.

There is no difference in the authenticity between Sunna and the Qur'ān. Just as the Qur'ān was received through the consensus of the companions and verbal mass transmission, the Sunna was received through their consensus and practical mass transmission. And like the Qur'ān, it has been proven through the consensus of Muslims in every era.

If the essence of this religion were to be captured in a single word, then according to Qur'ānic terminology, it would be *servitude* to God. This signifies humility and a deep sense of lowliness before Him. When this servitude emerges from a genuine recognition of Allāh Almighty, it leads a person to bow before Him with profound love and reverent fear. In reality, this servitude is an inner state. It is reflected in remembering God, expressing gratitude to Him, fearing His displeasure, being sincere towards Him, placing trust in Him, and accepting His will with contentment. These are the inward manifestations of servitude. Outwardly, it is expressed through acts of worship such as bowing and prostration, glorifying and praising God, supplication, and offering sacrifices.

Since human existence also has a practical dimension, this servitude does not remain confined to the inner state. When it extends to the realm of action, it encompasses not only worship but also obedience. At that stage, it requires a person to live as a true servant of God—both inwardly and outwardly.

In the relationship between the servant and the Lord, when this *servitude* lays down its foundations, prescribes rituals, defines its limits and boundaries for fulfilling its demands in the world, it is referred to as *Religion (Dīn)* in the language of the Qurʾān.

The form of religion that God Almighty has clarified to humankind through His prophets is referred to in the Qurʾān as *the true religion (dīn al-haqq)*. It instructs them to uphold it correctly and to implement it completely in their lives, without causing any divisions or dissensions within it.

For this servitude, the foundations of faith and ethics mentioned in God's religion are termed *Wisdom (Ḥikmah)*, while its rituals and its limits and restrictions are referred to as *The Law (Kitāb)*. Another term for it is *Sharīʿah*, meaning the same as law in our everyday language.

Ḥikmah has always been the same, but *Sharīʿah*, due to evolution and changes in human civilization, has varied significantly. A study of divine literature shows that mostly *Sharīʿah* is discussed in the Torah, and *Ḥikmah* in the Gospel. Psalms is a prelude to this Wisdom in the form of glorification of God Almighty, and the Qurʾān was revealed as a literary masterpiece embodying both *Ḥikmah* and *Kitāb*, and as a comprehensive scripture of warnings and glad tidings.

The term *Ḥikma* was adopted to describe two fundamental areas of discourse:

1. Faith & Beliefs
2. Morals & Morality

The topics outlined under *Kitāb* are:

1. The law of worship.
2. The law of family and social life.
3. The law of politics.
4. The Economic Law.
5. The law of calling to faith *(Da'wa)*.
6. The law of *Jihād*.
7. Fixed and Discretionary Punishments.
8. Dietary Guidelines.
9. Customs and Etiquette.
10. Oaths and their expiation.

This is religion in its entirety. Those envoys who brought this religion are known as Prophets *(Nabī)*. From the Qur'ān, it is learned that among them, some were also bestowed with the office of Messengership *(Risāla)* alongside Prophethood *(Nubuwwa)*.

Nubuwwa refers to the phenomenon in which a human being is chosen to receive revelation in order to convey the truth to people. He gives glad tidings of reward in the Hereafter to those who accept it and warns those who reject it of adverse consequences. The Qur'ān describes this role as one of warning *(Indhār)* and glad tidings *(Bashāra)*

Risāla on the other hand, is when such a person, endowed with the office of prophethood, is further entrusted with the role of being God's judgment upon his nation. If they reject him, then God's decree is carried out in this world through him, and the dominance of truth is practically established over them.

This happens in such a way that God Almighty selects these Messengers *(Rasūl)* for the manifestation of His reward and punishment and then, before the Day of Judgment, enacts a minor Day of Judgment through them in this world. The Messenger's addressees are informed that if they remain steadfast in their covenant with God, they will receive the reward, and if they deviate, they will face the consequences in this world itself.

The result is that the Messenger's presence among his people becomes a sign of God for them, and they see God, as it were, walking and administering justice on earth with them. Along with this, the Messengers are commanded to preach the truth they have witnessed with their own eyes—with utmost conviction—and to deliver God's guidance to the people without any additions or omissions, and with absolute certainty.

According to the Qur'ān, this is establishing the testimony *(Shahāda)*. When this testimony is established, it becomes the basis for divine judgment in both this world and the hereafter. Thus, God Almighty grants dominance to these Messengers and unleashes His punishment upon the deniers of their message.

In addition to the Messengers, the office of testimony was also bestowed upon the descendants of Prophet Abraham (PBUH). From this perspective, the Qur'ān describes them as a community positioned between God's Messenger and the people, entrusted with bearing witness to the truth. It further states that they were chosen in the same way that God Almighty selects certain individuals for Prophethood and Messengership.

Along with the prophets and messengers, God Almighty generally also revealed His scriptures. According to the Qur'ān, the purpose of these revelations is to serve as a standard for distinguishing truth from falsehood. They enable people to resolve their disputes and establish justice by adhering to the truth.

This chain of prophethood and messengership started with Adam (PBUH) and concluded with Muhammad, the Messenger of God (PBUH). After his departure from this world, the doors to revelation and inspiration have been permanently closed, and prophethood has been terminated. Consequently, the responsibility of Warning (*Indhār*) to keep people steadfast on religion now lies with the scholars of this Umma until the Day of Judgment.

The name of this religion is *Islam,* and God Almighty has declared in His Book that no other religion will be accepted from humanity.

Just as the term *Islam* refers to the entire religion, it is sometimes also used to describe the external, visible aspects of Islam. In this outward aspect, Islam consists of the following five practices:

1. Testifying that there is no deity except God and that Muhammad (PBUH) is His Messenger.
2. Establishing prayer *(Ṣalāh)*.
3. Paying Charity *(Zakāt)*.
4. Observing the fasts of Ramaḍān.
5. Performing Pilgrimage to the House of God *(Hajj)*.

The inner core of religion is faith. According to the details mentioned in the Qurʾān, it also consists of five things:

1. Belief in God.
2. Belief in the Angels.
3. Belief in the Prophets.
4. Belief in the Books.
5. Belief in the Day of Judgment.

When this faith, in terms of its essence, takes root in the heart and becomes firmly established, its very existence demands the following:

1. Righteous deeds, and
2. Exhorting others to truth and perseverance *(Tawāṣī bi-l-ḥaqq and Tawāṣī bi-ṣ-ṣabr)*.

Righteous deeds mean every act that results from the purifica- tion of ethics. The foundations of righteous deeds are rooted in reason and innate human nature, and God's *Sharīʿah* has been revealed to guide mankind toward them.

The meanings of *Tawāṣī bi-l-ḥaqq* and *Tawāṣī bi-ṣ-ṣabr* are advising one another, within one's surroundings, to uphold the truth and remain steadfast in it.

The Qurʾān also refers to this as enjoining what is right *(Amr bi-l-maʿrūf)* and forbidding what is wrong *(Nahy ʿani-l-munkar)*. In other words, the things recognized as good by intellect and human nature should be promoted in one's immediate surroundings, and things considered as wrong should be discouraged. These are the obligations of faith in normal circumstances. However, the challenges of the world may give rise to situations that call for three additional responsibilities:

1. Migration *(Hijra)*,

2. Support *(Nuṣra)*, and

3. Upholding Justice *(Qiyām bi-l-qisṭ).*

If a believer faces a situation where remaining steadfast in the worship of God risks their life, or if they are persecuted to the point where practicing and expressing their faith becomes impossible, their faith obligates them to leave such a place and relocate to a place where they can openly practice their religion. The Qur'ān refers to this as Migration *(Hijra)* and issues a stern warning of hellfire for those who, after the Prophet's call, find themselves in such circumstances yet fail to fulfill this obligation.

Similarly, if for the propagation or protection of religion there arises a need for some action, then faith demands that one supports the religion with their life and wealth. According to the terminology of the Qur'ān, this is the Support *(Nuṣra)* of God, and it asserts that if at any moment such a demand arises, then nothing in this world should be dearer to a believer than meeting this demand.

Moreover, if in any religious or worldly affair, one's emotions, prejudices, interests, or desires attempt to divert one from the path of justice, then the same faith demands that not only should a believer remain steadfast on justice and truth but also, if the situation demands testimony, he should be willing to risk his life to fulfill this demand. Speak the truth, submit to the truth, administer justice, bear witness to justice, and never choose anything other than justice in belief and action. The Qur'ān utilizes the phrase Establishing Justice *(Qiyām bi-l-qisṭ)* for this.

The objective of this religion, as outlined in the Qur'ān, is Purification *(Tazkiya).* This refers to the process of purifying both the individual and collective aspects of human life from impurities, while nurturing thoughts and actions in the right direction. The Qur'ān consistently emphasizes that the ultimate goal for humanity is to attain the highest level of paradise, and the key to reaching this position is the purification of oneself in this world. Therefore, the central purpose of religion is purification. Prophets were sent for this very purpose, and the entire revelation of religion serves to guide humanity toward achieving this goal and reaching the ultimate success.

The attitude that followers of this religion should adopt in practicing it is Excellence *(Iḥsān)*. *Iḥsān* means to perform any task in the best possible manner. Its expression is such that a person worships God Almighty as if they are seeing Him. And if they cannot see Him, then they are fully aware that their Lord is always watching them.

PART 1

THE WISDOM

(Al-Ḥikma)

FAITH & BELIEFS

F aith *(Īmān)* is a religious term that refers to the complete and unwavering acceptance of something in the heart. At its core, faith is the belief in God. When a person submits their heart and mind to God with the utmost devotion and contentment, they are considered a believer in the terminology of the Qurʾān. This is the true essence of faith. Therefore, the Qurʾān emphasizes that a person's words and actions must align with their faith. As a result, every good deed is regarded as a distinct characteristic of faith and an essential attribute of the believers.

There is no doubt that in the eye of the law, every person who verbally acknowledges Islam is a believer. His faith cannot be deemed lesser or greater. However, as far as true faith is concerned, it is not at all a stagnant thing. It grows with the remembrance of God, the recitation of His verses, and the manifestation of His signs in oneself and the universe. The

Holy Qur'ān has likened it to a tree whose roots are deeply entrenched in the earth and whose branches spread across the heavens.

The same applies to the decrease of faith. If a person starts acting against the demands of his faith instead of continuously increasing it with beneficial knowledge and righteous actions, then his faith also decreases, and in some situations, it can completely vanish.

Thus, it is evident that faith and action are both essential and inseparable. Just as actions are necessary along with faith, faith is also necessary along with actions. The Qur'ān has consistently presented this as a fundamental condition for salvation. This belief consists of believing in the following five things:

1. Belief in God,
2. Belief in angels,
3. Belief in Prophets,
4. Belief in scriptures,
5. Belief in the Day of Judgment.

Belief in God

Allāh is the name of the entity who is the creator of the earth, the heavens, and all creatures. This name has been exclusive to the Lord of the worlds from the beginning. Even before Prophet Muhammad (PBUH), this name was used in the pre-Islamic Arab society with the same meaning. It is one of the remnants of the Abrahamic religion that was inherited by the Arabs.

Acknowledging this entity is something that has been innately placed within humans since eternity. The Qur'ān states that this matter took the form of a covenant.

The Qurʾān mentions this covenant as an actual event. Humans were sent to this world for a test; thus, the memory of this event has been erased from their conscious minds, but its reality is engraved in their subconscious and deeply embedded in their minds, a truth that cannot be erased.

Therefore, when there are no external hindrances and a person is reminded, they are naturally drawn to it. This is much like a child instinctively reaching for its mother, even though the child has no recollection of being born, yet leaps toward her with a sense of familiarity, as if it already knows her. Similarly, the individual feels that acknowledging God satisfies a deep, inherent need within them. Once embraced, this acknowledgment aligns with and fulfills all the emotional and psychological demands of their being.

The Qurʾān declares that the human soul's testimony regarding God's lordship is so definitive that every individual is accountable to God based on this testimony alone.

In addition to innate guidance, humans have been endowed with the ability to infer certain truths beyond their direct sensory experiences, based on what they see, hear, and feel.

A simple example is the Law of Gravitation. When an apple falls from a tree, it hits the ground. Lifting a stone from the earth requires effort. Climbing stairs is more difficult than descending them. The moon and stars move in their orbits across the sky. For centuries, humans observed these phenomena until one day, Newton revealed that they were all governed by the law of gravitation. This law itself is invisible, yet today it is universally accepted as a scientific fact.

This acceptance comes from the fact that the theory aligns with all known facts, explains every observation, and no alternative theory has been proposed that accounts for these events as comprehensively as the law of gravitation does.

It is clear that this is an inference of the unseen from the seen. When a person uses this capacity to study themselves and the universe around them, their study also testifies to the same truth hidden within them.

So, they observe that every object in this world is a miraculous manifestation of creative elegance; there is profound significance, extraordinary care, wisdom, purpose, and astonishing order and arrangement; unparalleled geometry and mathematics, which cannot be explained by anything other than having a creator. This Creator is not a blind and deaf force, but a being of infinite wisdom and intelligence. For if the manifestation of power did not arise from a knowing and wise source, it would amount to mere coercion. But clearly, that is not the case. Rather, it shows extreme suitability, tremendous harmony, generates extraordinary benefits and peculiar variations, which could not arise from any blind and deaf force.

Although these evidences were sufficient, to provide conclusive proof to humanity, God ordained that the beginning of human history take place through a person who heard God's voice, saw His angels, and departed from this world after bearing witness to the reality through direct observation, so that his knowledge might be transferred from generation to generation, ensuring that the concept of God never becomes alien to any era of human life, any region of the earth, any community, any generation, or any race.

In addition to sending Adam and Eve into the world as the first human beings, God established a system through which, for a certain period, their descendants could witness the acceptance or rejection of their faith and deeds. This system enabled them to experience divine judgment in a tangible form, thereby making them participants in the same testimony as their parents. This verification occurred when people presented offerings to God. As a sign of acceptance, fire would descend from the sky and consume the offerings. This miraculous event provided clear evidence of divine approval for every person of that time.

This makes it evident that the existence of God is a self-evident truth that humans have inherited from their ancestors, and which both soul and matter testify to with their existence.

But what is the nature of God? What are His attributes? What are the laws He has set for Himself? If a person wishes to attain knowledge of their Lord, these questions inevitably arise in their mind. This knowledge is essential for faith. When the Qur'ān demands faith in God, it also provides answers to these questions. What are these answers? We will clarify this here.

Essence *(Dhāt)*

The Qur'ān has made it abundantly clear about the *dhāt* of God Almighty that in no way can it come within the human scope of perception. This is because the creator of the means of perception can certainly encompass and comprehend them, but these means cannot in any way encompass the One who encompasses everything.

Attributes

The attributes of God Almighty, however, to some extent, do come within human grasp. This is because some aspects related to attributes, no matter how insignificant, are also present in humans.

God Almighty has granted us a share of His knowledge, awareness, power, lordship, mercy, and wisdom. By analogy, we can form—at least to some extent—an idea of these divine attributes.

Therefore, when the Qur'ān states that He is the Creator, the All-Powerful, the Most Merciful and Compassionate, the All-Knowing and Wise, the Ever-Living and Self-Sustaining, the First and the Last, the Apparent and the Hidden, it indeed establishes a concept of God's attributes.

When contemplating these attributes, it is essential to appreciate their aspect of elegance, as true power is only commendable when coupled with mercy, generosity, and justice. In the same way, anger, vengeance, and wrath are praiseworthy when directed against oppression and aggression. Mercy, forgiveness, and generosity are likewise worthy of praise when applied appropriately. The Holy Qur'ān highlights this dimension of elegance by describing God's attributes as the Self-Sufficient with the Praiseworthy, the All-Knowing with the Wise and the Almighty with the Forgiving.

Similarly, it should also be noted that any concept of God Almighty that is established cannot be devoid of majesty, elegance, and perfection. For example, attributes of perfection are the Indivisible, the Unique, the rock of refuge. The Pure, the Source of Peace, and the Giver of Security are attributes of elegance and attributes of majesty include the King, the Almighty, the Compeller.

In the human heart, attributes of majesty inspire fear, reverence, and laudation, and attributes of elegance inspire admiration, hope, and love. Then, attributes of majesty are more obvious to the senses, while attributes of elegance are nearer to the intellect and the heart.

When considering the Creator, the dominance of attributes of elegance is felt; but when confronting the human ego, the aspect of majesty becomes prominent. Man rushes towards God out of fear and tries to seek refuge in the embrace of His attributes of elegance.

The Holy Qur'ān, when it says all the good names belong to Him, means that every name that expresses God's majesty, elegance, and perfection is good and can be used to call upon Him.

The attributes of perfection of God Almighty are significant because they highlight His greatness. When one correctly conceives these attributes, as a result, one believes in a God who is unique, incomparable, and unmatched; a rock of refuge for all; the sole owner of the earth and the skies and everything in between; whose sovereignty has no partner; whose mechanism of creation has no co-sharer; nothing is hidden from His sight; no matter is beyond His command; everything is in need of Him, and He needs none; inanimate objects, plants, animals all prostrate before Him and are engaged in His glorification and praise; His power is limitless, His extent unbounded, and His will operates in every particle of the universe; He can annihilate and recreate whatever and whenever He wills; honor and disgrace are in His hands; all are transient, He alone is eternal; He is beyond all comprehension, yet closer than the jugular vein; His knowledge and power encompass everything; He knows the secrets of the hearts; His decree prevails over all wills, and His command is above all commands; He is free from all faults, aloof from all evils, and absolved of all accusations.

Among these attributes of perfection, the most important

is the oneness of God Almighty. The Holy Qur'ān has expli-
cated it with utmost emphasis and clarity. So much so that the
last chapter of this heavenly scripture ends on the Surah that
instructs the Prophet to openly declare that God is One, the
sustainer of all, He is neither a father nor a son of anyone, and
there is none comparable to Him.

The significance of monotheism is precisely why the Qur'ān
declares that without it, no human deed is acceptable, and
with it, there remains hope for the forgiveness of all sins. For a
person who believes in monotheism cannot persist in sin with
rebellion, nor is he deprived of the grace of repentance and
divine forgiveness after committing a sin. Inevitably, he turns
back to his Lord, thereby securing for himself the entitlement
to pardon and forgiveness before the Day of Judgment.

The arguments for monotheism presented in the Qur'ān are
extremely appealing and based on established facts of knowledge and reason. It is enough to say that no one has any evidence
for making anyone a partner in God's divinity. The Qur'ān has,
on more than one occasion, called upon its audience to provide
any rational or scriptural proof for their claims—if they can,
they should certainly do so. Whether there is a partner to God
or not, the primary witness can only be God Himself, and the
only way to know God's testimony is through His revealed
scriptures and those traditions and accounts that have been
transmitted to humanity generation by generation through His
Prophets and Messengers. In them, there is no endorsement of
polytheism.

God's Way

The manner and method God Almighty deals with humans
are referred to in the Qur'ān as the Way of God *(Sunnat Allāh)*.

God Almighty declares that these protocols are immutable, with absolutely no changes occurring within them. Thus, just as knowledge of His attributes is essential for understanding God, knowledge of these divine sunna is also essential. These sunna are as follows:

1. **Trial:** God Almighty has created this world as a place of trial. This test encompasses all of humanity like a universal law. Through it, what is inherent in human nature becomes manifest; the mysteries of the self are unveiled, and the levels of knowledge and action are revealed. The Qur'ān states that the creation of life and death is for the Lord to see who behaves rebelliously and who lives life according to His liking. Undoubtedly, God is omniscient, but He has set a sunna that matters of reward and punishment will not be based merely on His knowledge. This test has been initiated for this purpose.

   The conditions of hardship and comfort, poverty and wealth, sorrow, and happiness that humans experience in this world are all under this law. Through these, God tests His servants and distinguishes between the genuine and the fake. He tests gratitude when He endows someone with wealth and status and tests patience when He subjects someone to poverty and hardship.

2. **Guidance and Misguidance:** In this trial, it is demanded from humans to avoid misguidance and choose the path of guidance for themselves. The Qur'ān explains that this guidance is innately placed within human nature. Once they attain intellectual awareness, the signs in the heavens and the earth draw them toward it. If a person values this guidance, benefits from it, and is thankful for this

blessing of God, it is God's sunna to increase this light for him, enhance his desire for more guidance, and as a result, enable him to benefit from the guidance brought by the Prophets. If a person deliberately turns away from this innate guidance, neglects the use of reason, and knowingly deviates from the truth, then—according to the Qur'ān—such a person is guilty of injustice and defiant disobedience. God does not guide those who persist in wrongdoing and defiance but leaves them to wander in the darkness of misguidance.

3. **Testing Beyond Endurance:** The *Sharī'ah* revealed through the Prophets does not command humans anything beyond their endurance. A consistent standard in all acts ordained by God is that no burden greater than one's capacity is placed upon individuals, and any command given considers human nature and capacities.

   Thus, in this *Sharī'ah*, there is no accountability for mistakes, misunderstandings, and unintended shortcomings, and it only demands that people comply with its commands earnestly and honestly in their outward and inner selves. However, this does not mean that when people choose rebellion, God never places any hardship upon them. The Qur'ān reveals that such hardship is indeed inflicted—for discipline and moral training, for punishment, to show people the consequences of their evil deeds, and to reveal their helplessness before God.

4. **Rise and Fall of Nations:** Under the law of trial mentioned earlier, just as God selects individuals for tests of patience and gratitude, He also selects nations. As a result of this selection, when a nation attains a position of honor

and prominence, God does not change its status until it debases itself in knowledge and morals. This is God's unchanging sunna. According to this practice, when — after repeated warnings — God decrees humiliation and downfall for a nation, that decision cannot be deferred, and no power in the world can assist that nation against Him. The entire history of humanity bears testimony to this practice regarding the rise and fall of nations.

5. **Divine Support:** When God entrusts a mission to an individual or a group and commands its fulfillment, He also supports them. This mission could be of preaching or warfare. God has made it obligatory upon Himself to aid the believers in accomplishing such missions. This help is not arbitrary; it follows a certain principle. God has outlined this principle in the Qurʾān. His servants receive this support according to this principle.

6. **Repentance and Forgiveness:** When a human commits a sin, there is room for repentance and seeking forgiveness. The rule in this matter is that if the person repents immediately after committing a sin, God surely forgives him. However, He does not accept the repentance of those who dwell in sins all their life and start seeking repentance when death looms over them. Similarly, the repentance of those who knowingly deny the truth is not accepted if they persist in their denial until death.

7. **Reward and Punishment:** The reward and punishment after death is an inevitable certainty. However, the Qurʾān informs us that, at times, this outcome is also dispensed in this world. This dispensation serves as a precursor to the manifestation of God's ultimate judgment, which

will appear in its perfect and complete form on the Day of Resurrection. The forms of these outcomes, as specifically described by God Almighty, are:

a. Firstly, those who are seekers of this world, living and dying for it, and leading their lives completely indifferent to the hereafter, God Almighty settles their accounts in this world itself, giving them as He pleases and concludes their matters, letting them receive the fruits of their actions here only.

b. Secondly, after the Conclusive Establishment of the Truth through Messengers, the deniers face punishment in this world, while for the believers, God opens the doors of the blessings of the earth and the heavens.

c. Thirdly, for the progeny of Prophet Abraham (PBUH), there's a promise from God that if they stand firm on truth, they would achieve leadership among nations, and if they deviate, they would be removed from this position and subjected to humiliation and subjugation as punishment.

Belief in Angels

The beings through whom God communicates His commands to His creation are called angels. In the Qur'ān, the word used for them is *al-malā'ikah*, the plural of *malak*, meaning "messenger." Thus, the Qur'ān reveals that the connection between the celestial and terrestrial realms is established through their mediation, and they manage all affairs according to the decrees of God. Their role is such that the command given to them by God Himself is carried out among His creatures like that of a mere subordinate, without any exercise of their own will. They are the embodiment of obedience, constantly engaged in praising their Lord, and they do not deviate from His command in the slightest.

Belief in Prophets

The distinguished individuals through whom God arranged for the guidance of the children of Adam are called Prophets. They were humans but were chosen by God based on His knowledge and wisdom for this role. This is a divine gift, not attained through instruction, training, or learning. The Qurʾān tells us that the chosen ones are those who protect themselves from the temptations of the self and Satan, remain safe from sins, and are among the righteous and the best of their people.

God sent these Prophets to every community. He had promised Adam (PBUH) that He would send guidance to his progeny. This guidance was delivered to humanity through these Prophets. They received revelation from heaven and conveyed the truth to the people—giving glad tidings of good consequences to the believers and warning the disbelievers of the consequences of their denial.

The necessity of Prophets was not because humans could not recognize their creator or differentiate between good and evil. All these aspects are part of human nature and were imprinted in it from the first day of creation. Thus, the need arose not for making them aware of these facts but for two reasons:

1. to complete the guidance, meaning reminding humans of what is vaguely present in their nature and defining it clearly with necessary details;

2. and to complete the Argument *(Itmam al-Hujja)[5]*, meaning to awaken humans from their negligence and, after appealing to reason and intellect, to present further evidence through these Prophets that clarifies the truth to such an extent that no excuse remains.

With the advent of Muhammad, the Messenger of God (PBUH), these two purposes were achieved globally and to the fullest extent, hence the chain of Prophethood has been terminated. The Qur'ān has declared that he is the last Prophet, and after him, no Prophet or Messenger will come.

Recognizing these prophets is not difficult for a person with a sound natural disposition. If a person's heart and mind are truly awake, then both

> *"the face and voice of the Prophet*
> *are miracles in themselves."*

(روۓ وآواز پیمبر معجزہ ست)

However, God also grants them clear signs so that even if the opponents do not verbally admit, they are left with no choice but to believe in their truthfulness. The Qur'ān tells us that these clear signs are given to every Prophet according to their era and circumstances. Among these, some are mentioned here.

1. A Prophet generally comes as the fulfillment of the prophecy of a previous Prophet, thus not being an unfamiliar figure. People are acquainted with him and await his arrival. It's explicitly stated regarding Jesus (PBUH) that John the Baptist had announced his coming, in Jerusalem before his advent.

---

5. This book refers to this phenomenon as the "Conclusive Establishment of the Truth."

The good news of the coming of the Messenger of God (PBUH) is mentioned in both the Torah and the Gospel. In fact, one of the major objectives stated for the advent of Jesus was to announce the coming of the Unlettered Prophet.

The Qur'ān has presented this as a decisive proof of its truthfulness, stating that the scholars of Israelites recognize him as a longing father would recognize his promised and long-awaited son. This meant that they were well aware of the Messenger of God (PBUH).

2. What a Prophet delivers as the word of God is free from contradictions. No human intellect, however brilliant—be it Socrates, Plato, Kant, Einstein, Ghālib, Iqbāl, Rāzī, or Zamakhsharī—can claim this level of consistency in their works.

Yet, The Qur'ān confidently asserts about itself that it does not contain even the slightest inconsistency in thought or concept. After all, can anyone—speaking over many years, in different situations, and on such a wide range of topics—do so in a way that, when compiled, forms a fully cohesive and harmonious body of discourse? One that is free from conflicting ideas, changes in mood, or shifts in perspective? This remarkable quality is found in the Qur'ān alone.

3. God bestows miracles and supernatural events upon prophets. The extraordinary miracles given to Moses (PBUH) and Jesus (PBUH) have been explicitly mentioned in the Qur'ān as indications of their Prophethood.

These miracles cannot be dismissed as mere sorcery or an expert display of specialized knowledge or skill, because no one grasps the essence of such knowledge and skills better than the experts themselves—and they, too, are compelled to acknowledge their own limitations when confronted with these miracles.

The miracle given to the Prophet (PBUH) in this regard is the Qur'ān. Experts of the Arabic language and literary tradition, when they read it, distinctly feel that it cannot be the word of a human. Therefore, on several occasions, it has directly challenged its audiences that if they truly believe it is not the word of God but fabricated by Muhammad (PBUH), then they should produce even a single chapter of similar quality. If a member of their community, as they claim, without any scholarly or literary background, can manage this task, then they should have no difficulty in doing so.

This Book of God remains with us even today, nearly fourteen centuries since its revelation. Over this period, the world has transformed dramatically. Humanity has crafted and then discarded countless ideologies, while its perspectives on itself and the universe have shifted repeatedly. Societies have explored diverse paths, passed through phases of acceptance and rejection of countless ideas and theories—and ultimately reached a certain point. Yet this Book—foretelling many subjects that later became focal points of human knowledge, remains unique in all of literature: unchanged and as authoritative as it was fourteen hundred years ago. Knowledge and reason, once awed by its insight, continue today to recognize their limitations before it. Each statement within still holds its full significance, and despite remarkable advancements in understanding, the world finds no grounds for amendments or alterations to its words.

4. God informs a Prophet about certain matters that would be impossible for any human to know. An example of this is the divine prophecies in revelation, which astonishingly came true precisely. Some of these prophecies are found in the Qur'ān and some in traditions. Every student of the Qur'ān is aware of the prophecy regarding the dominance of the Messenger of God (PBUH) in the Arabian Peninsula, the conquest of Mecca, and people entering God's religion in droves. The prophecy of the Romans' victory after their defeat by the Persians was truly remarkable and without precedent.

When this prophecy was made, according to the words of the author of *The Decline and Fall of the Roman Empire*, Edward Gibbon,

> *"..no prophecy could be more distant from its accomplishment, since the first twelve years of Heraclius announced the approaching dissolution of the empire"*
>
> *(Chapter XLVI: Troubles in Persia-Part III, Page 1904)*

Yet, it was fulfilled at the appointed time, and in March 628, the Roman ruler returned to Constantinople in such glory that his chariot was drawn by four elephants, and countless people were present outside the imperial palace with lamps and olive branches, waiting to welcome their hero.

5. Prophets who are granted the status of Messengers act as representatives of God's judgment on earth, determining

the fate of their people before departing from this world. When these Messengers uphold their covenant with God, they are rewarded; if they deviate, they face punishment in this life. Thus, their lives become a living sign of divine authority, and it is as though people witness God walking, acting, and making judgments among them. This serves as the foundation for God's decree regarding their nations, both in this world and in the hereafter. God grants these Messengers dominance and sends His punishment upon those who reject their message.

God's command regarding these Prophets is that they be obeyed. God Himself has made it clear in His Book that a Prophet is not just a focal point of devotion but also of obedience. He does not come just so people can recognize him as a Prophet or Messenger and then be done with it. His role is not merely that of an adviser or preacher, but as a guide whose obedience is mandatory. The purpose of his advent is to ensure that the guidance he provides in all aspects of life is followed without question. Moreover, this obedience is not a mere formality. The Qur'ān demands that it be followed with a spirit of devotion, complete sincerity, love, and utmost respect and reverence.

Belief in the Scriptures

Just as Prophets were sent for the guidance of humanity, God Almighty also revealed His books along with them. These books were revealed so that guidance from God could remain in writing and in His own words among people, to serve as a measure for truth and falsehood. This would allow people to resolve their disputes by referring to it, thereby establishing justice in matters of religion.

The existing collection of earlier scriptures, the Bible, suggests that some form of divine book or revelation was given to every Prophet. The Qurʾān mentions the Torah and the Gospel in the same way it mentions the Scriptures of Abraham. All of these are divine books, and God calls for belief in the overall message of these scriptures without discrimination.

Among these, four books hold extraordinary significance: the Torah, the Psalms, the Gospel, and the Qurʾān. The Torah was revealed to Moses (PBUH), the Psalms to David (PBUH), and the Gospel to Jesus (PBUH). The Qurʾān was revealed to God's last Prophet, Muhammad, (PBUH). Of all divine texts, the Qurʾān stands uniquely as the only book we can affirm with certainty to exist today exactly as it was revealed—unaltered, in its original language and structure.

Belief in the Day of Judgment

The belief in the Day of Judgment holds extraordinary importance among the truths that religion demands to be believed. This belief is fundamental in the message of the Prophets, peace be upon them. The foundation of all laws, goodness, and virtue rests on this belief. The basis of Prophethood and Messengerhood is established on this. A prophet is a prophet because he brings news of this great announcement. A messenger is a messenger because he comes with its message. The Qurʾān is a scripture of warning and glad tidings for this Day of Judgment. It tells people that just as you wake up after sleeping; just as rain falls on the dead earth and it comes to life before your very eyes; just as you were nothing but then became living beings from a drop of water, similarly, one day you will be raised from the graves. Your Lord will not face any difficulty in this. Its recipients consider it improbable and say, "Who will revive these decayed bones?" It replies, "He who produced them the first time will revive them." Reviving is as easy for Him as speaking a word.

The evidence, signs, situations, and stages of this are clearly described.

- **Evidence**

   1. The first thing is the awareness of good and evil within a person. This awareness brings forth an inner guardian, an ever-watchful presence within the conscience, cautioning against wrongdoing. It is like a small court established within every person, offering impartial judgments on each occasion. Whether or not a person accepts this verdict, he indeed hears it after every lapse in thought, knowledge, and action, until, if unchecked, the darkness of one's deeds eventually overwhelms the heart, rendering it spiritually blind and deaf. This is the internal testimony placed within humans, known in the Qur'ān as the testimony of *The Self-Accusing Soul (al-nafs al-lawwāmah)*. The Qur'ān informs humans that they are not unchecked beasts that do whatever they wish without being questioned. You must understand that just as a minor day of judgment prevails within you, similarly, a grand day of judgment will inevitably occur for the entire universe, where you will stand accountable before your Lord, and judgment will be passed based on what you have done. Denying this truth is to deny your own self and confront your conscience with deception.

   2. The second thing is the human nature that desires justice

and detests oppression. There is no doubt that despite this, humans commit oppression. However, the reason is not that humans cannot differentiate between oppression and justice or that they love oppression, however, overcome by emotions and desires, they lose the natural balance within themselves. Every person knows that humans might break into others' homes, yet they would never want anyone breaking into their own; they kill others but never likes anyone to kill them or any of their loved ones; they might cheat others in measurement but would never accept being cheated. Even thieves, murderers, and deceivers, when questioned, would acknowledge that such acts are wrong and should be eliminated.

Therefore, no sane person can agree that good and evil should be regarded the same and treated equally. The Qur'ān emphasizes these truths and questions those who deny the Day of Judgment: "Shall We then treat the obedient and the criminals alike? What is wrong with you? How do you judge?"

3. The third important point is the inherent incompleteness of humans and the universe. When we examine them closely, we see a clear reflection of the immense power and wisdom of their Creator in every detail. Every element displays profound purpose, unmatched organization, flawless mathematical precision, extraordinary attention to detail, and boundless creative elegance that astonishes the human mind and intellect. Yet, when viewed as a whole, both humanity and the universe appear to lack ultimate fulfillment, giving an impression

of incompleteness and lack of purpose. This observation leads to two possible interpretations:

a. To regard this grand design of existence as purposeless—reducing it to a trivial, meaningless play without any real significance.

b. To interpret it in the context of a coming Day of Judgment and the eternal kingdom of God, as proclaimed by the Prophets, peace be upon them.

The rational and intellectual conclusion is evident for anyone willing to reflect.

4. The fourth thing is the divine attributes, whose signs are evident in every particle of the universe. Among these, particularly noteworthy are the attributes of lordship and mercy. After seeing the extraordinary care taken by the Lord of the worlds for human sustenance, how can any sensible person believe that his Creator will leave him unaccountable and how can it be expected from the Merciful and Compassionate God that He would not punish those who have made the world a home of oppression and aggression? Qur'ān has repeatedly directed attention to the fact that the Day of Judgment is necessitated by the mercy, lordship, power, and wisdom of God Almighty. After believing in God, no one can deny it.

5. The fifth point is the manifestation of God's judgment in this world. This occurred through certain prophets who were elevated to the position of messengers. God granted these Messengers extraordinary miracles, supported them with the Holy Spirit, and, through them, established a form of judgment in this world prior to

the final Day of Judgment. This was intended to validate the concept of the Hereafter in a manner akin to how scientific facts are proven through experiments. Consequently, no one would have any excuse to present before God.

The method adopted was that these messengers delivered the call of truth and declared that they had come to their people as God's judgment on earth. The reward or punishment for faith and deeds, as proclaimed, would be realized in this world for their nation. Just as physical laws yield consistent outcomes, God's moral law would also take effect, following the Conclusive Establishment of Truth through them. Thus, those who accepted their call would attain salvation in both this world and the Hereafter, prevailing over their adversaries. Conversely, those who rejected the message would face disgrace, and God's punishment would descend upon them.

Every prediction made at the time and for every nation was seemingly impossible and unbelievable, but each time it was fulfilled in such a manner that people saw God administering justice, and the earth and skies were filled with His majesty.

The Qur'ān indicates that the final instance of this divine judgment took place in the seventh century CE through Muhammad, the Messenger of God (PBUH). This event holds exceptional significance in human history because it unfolded in documented historical times. Its details are thoroughly preserved, allowing anyone to witness its phases by examining the records of history.

- **Signs**

  When will this day come? The Qur'ān has made it clear that no one knows except God. Its time is only known to Him, and He does not inform any of His Prophets or angels about it. Its signs and indications, however, have been mentioned in the Qur'ān, ḥadīth, and ancient scriptures. Some of these signs are of a general nature, while the nature of others pertains to specific events and occurrences.None of the first kind of signs have been mentioned in the Qur'ān. They are mentioned in traditions. Of the second kind of signs, only one thing has been mentioned in the Qur'ān, and that is the emergence of Gog and Magog. Therefore, this is the definite sign. Other than this, of the signs that are generally mentioned, some have already appeared, and the rest will necessarily appear if there is no mistake in attributing them to Prophet Muhammad (PBUH).

- **Events**

  How will the Day of Judgment be established? Its details are described in several places in the Qur'ān. What will happen to the earth and the heavens, to the sun, the moon, the stars, and the planets? What fate will befall the creatures living on earth? How will people rise from their graves and gather before their Lord? The Qur'ān presents vivid depictions of these events throughout its chapters. A study of pre-Islamic *(Jāhiliyya)* literature reveals that the Arabs of that time favored imagery—particularly similes—over abstract metaphors, which the Qur'ān also powerfully employs in portraying these realities. The Qur'ān has taken this into consideration and has depicted the commotion of the Day of Judgment in such a way that its reader feels as though they are witnessing it unfold before their very eyes. The sequence of events that emerges is as follows:

1. People will be going about their lives with complete peace of mind—some on the road, some in the market, some in gatherings, and others at home. It won't even cross their minds that the very order of the world is about to be turned upside down. Suddenly, the trumpet will be blown, and the earthquake of the Day of Judgment will erupt.

   What the earth's populace will go through has been portrayed in multiple places in the Qur'ān. It shows that when relentless quakes follow one after another, the condition of the earth will be like a boat swaying violently under the pounding of waves. Hearts will tremble, eyes will be filled with terror, and people will be so bewildered and overwhelmed that it will seem as though the horrors of God's punishment have driven everyone to madness

2. This is the time when the order of the world will begin to disintegrate. A cataclysmic convulsion will sweep across the universe, causing mountains to crumble, seas to erupt, and galaxies and celestial bodies to crash into one another. Every corner of existence will witness such chaos that the human mind cannot conceive it, nor can words adequately describe it. This chain of events will last for a period—the duration of which only God knows.

3. After this, the stage that the Qur'ān describes as *The*

Recreation will begin. Gradually, from this disorder, a new system of nature will emerge. All celestial bodies—the earth, sun, moon, stars, and billions of stars and planets that constitute galaxies—will transform into a new heaven and earth with new laws and regulations. The Qurʾān states that at this moment the trumpet will be blown again, making all people rise and, emerging from their graves, present themselves before the Lord of the Universe.

- **Stages**

  The stages that humans will pass through to reach that day, and the places where they will be settled afterward, are also detailed in the Qurʾān. Humanity is steadily moving toward it. The first stage of this journey is death. After a brief span of worldly life, this stage inevitably arrives for every individual, and there is no escape from it. It can come in the morning or evening, before birth, or shortly after; in childhood, youth, or old age—whenever it pleases. Each person must surrender to it, whether willingly or reluctantly.

  The Qurʾān describes that a person's true self, referred to as the *nafs*, is an existence distinct and independent from their corporeal life. At the moment of death, this *nafs* is separated from the body. A specific angel is assigned this responsibility, supported by a group of angels working under his command. This angel comes and formally takes the *nafs* into custody, much like a government official takes possession of something entrusted to them.

  The Qurʾān also mentions the dealings with a person

at this moment. After the Conclusive Establishment of Truth by the Prophets, the souls of their deniers are seized by angels who strike them, and it is made known to them at the time of death that they are now to face the punishment of disgrace. On the other hand, those who believe in the Messenger and are completely purified from disbelief, polytheism, oppression, and all forms of corruption, the angels greet them with peace and give them glad tidings of Paradise.

After that comes the stages known as the *Intermediate State (Barzakh)*, the *Gathering (Maḥshar)*, *Hell* and *Paradise*. *The Intermediate State* serves as a barrier where the souls of the deceased will remain until the Day of Judgment. In various traditions, the term *grave* is metaphorically used to describe this state. Here, humans will experience a form of life without a physical body. The consciousness, sensations, and experiences of the soul in this state will bear some resemblance to what is experienced during dreams.

The Qurʾān informs us that for those whose situations are unequivocally clear—whether they are at the height of loyalty or are outright rebels and arrogant deniers—a form of punishment or reward will begin in this very realm. This is because there will be no need for their actions to be reviewed or their deeds to be judged.

The next station is *Maḥshar*. After the second blowing of the trumpet, all humans will rise to life again. This life will be with both soul and body. The Qurʾān has referred to it as the second life. In this, the worldly body of humans will be transformed into a body that will be suitable for living in all conditions of comfort and torment in God's eternal kingdom, but with the same personality as they are alive today.

All of humanity will be divided into three groups on that day:

    i. those who were foremost in accepting the truth,

    ii. the common righteous whose record of deeds will be given in their right hand,

    iii. and the criminals whose hands will be tied behind their back and their record of deeds be placed in their left hand.

This is the moment when the accounts will be taken, and witnesses will be presented for the Conclusive Establishment of the Truth. Prophets will also be called to testify. People's tongues, hands, feet, ears, eyes, and even the hair on their bodies will bear witness. After this, the verdict will be announced, and people will be dispatched to Hell or Paradise.

The Qur'ān states that Hell is the worst place to be. It will have the punishment of fire. This fire will scorch faces, disfigure them, peel off the skin, and reach the hearts. Criminals will have collars around their necks and chains on their feet, and everything will become a source of regret. Above all, people will be deprived of seeing God Almighty's radiant presence and of receiving His gaze of favor; He will not even turn to look at some of these criminals.

In contrast to Hell, Paradise is the dwelling place of the righteous. Its vastness is as extensive as the universe. It is a place of eternal bliss, where there is no concept of life followed by death, pleasure tainted by pain, happiness overshadowed by sorrow, tranquility disturbed by distress, ease interrupted by hardship, or blessings accompanied by curses. Instead, its comfort is everlasting, its delights are boundless, its days and nights are eternal, its peace is perpetual, its joy is undying, its elegance is eternal, and its perfection is infinite. God Almighty has provided therein such things for His servants which no eye has seen, no ear has heard, and no human heart has ever conceived.

MORALS & MORALITY

After faith, the most essential requirement of religion is the purification of one's character. This involves making one's actions pure in dealings with both the Creator and fellow beings, which is known as performing righteous deeds. All aspects of *Sharīʿah* stem from this foundational principle. There is no doubt that the *Sharīʿah* evolved in response to changing civilizations; faith and righteous deeds have always remained the essence of religion, untouched by any alteration. The Qurʾān makes it clear that anyone who comes to God with these two will be granted eternal paradise.

The Qurʾān also affirms that just as humans are endowed with eyes to see and ears to hear, they are also given a moral sense to discern right from wrong. This moral dimension is an intrinsic part of human existence, distinct from intellectual and physical existence. This innate ability to differentiate between good and evil suggests that the knowledge of what is good and what is bad was ingrained in human nature from the very beginning. This distinction is universally recognized: even the most corrupt individuals, when committing a wrong, initially feel the need to hide it. Similarly, people are naturally drawn to goodness, feel honored by it, and invariably establish systems of justice and fairness when forming societies.

This inherent awareness of right and wrong serves as evidence of a moral compass within. While people may sometimes devise justifications for their wrongdoings, they are aware, even in those moments, that these excuses contradict their innate nature. Thus, if someone else commits the same wrongdoing against them, they promptly recognize it as evil and protest unequivocally.

While interpretations of this divine guidance may vary based on individual perspectives, times, and circumstances, God Almighty has minimized the potential for major disagreements by clarifying good and evil through His Prophets. This guidance, preserved in the Qurʾān until the Day of Judgment, aligns with the moral understanding that individuals find within themselves. Human conscience, empirical knowledge, insights drawn from life's natural and physical laws, and intellectual reasoning all affirm this truth, resulting in a clear and definitive understanding of virtues and vices.

Basic Principles

For this purpose, God Almighty has established foundational principles for humanity: He commands people to act with justice and kindness, to spend on relatives, and forbids obscenities, detestable acts, and defiance. These principles are entirely natural and have always been central to God's religion. The Ten Commandments of the Torah are rooted in these principles, and the Qurʾān has structured its moral teachings around them as well. Here, we will explore these principles.

1. The first principle is justice. This means that the rights of every individual should be fully and impartially honored, regardless of whether the person is weak or powerful, and regardless of personal feelings. Justice requires that everyone receives what they are due without bias.

2. The second principle is *Kindness (ihsān)*. Kindness goes beyond justice and represents the height of moral elegance and perfection. It involves not only fulfilling others' rights but also adopting an attitude of generosity and selflessness. Kindness means giving others more than their due and being content with receiving less than one's own due. This fosters love, affection, selflessness, sincerity, gratitude, magnanimity, and benevolence within society, adding warmth and joy to life.

3. The third principle is spending on relatives. This is a specific form of kindness, recognizing the unique responsibilities toward family members. Relatives are entitled not only to fair and kind treatment but also have a rightful share in one's wealth. People should not allow their relatives to suffer in poverty or neglect but should strive, to the best of their ability, to meet their needs generously, just as they would for their own children.

In contrast, there are three things from which one is prohibited.

1. The first is obscenities, which encompass acts such as fornication, sodomy, and other similar behaviors.

2. The second is detestable acts—those actions universally regarded as wrong, consistently condemned throughout history, and so evidently harmful that they need no

further justification. Every sound religious, cultural, and civilizational tradition has deemed them wrong. The Qur'ān uses terms like *Munkar* and *Ithm* to describe these acts, emphasizing that they violate the rights of others.

3. The third is rebellious defiance, meaning a person misuses their power, strength, or influence for unjust gain, transgresses limits, and attempts to infringe upon the rights of others, whether those rights belong to the Creator or the creation.

Virtues and Vices

The Qur'ān has clarified virtues and vices in a well-defined manner, beginning and ending the discourse with the prohibition of associating partners with God. This style serves to underscore the significance of the subject. The belief in one God functions as a fortress for these virtues, safeguarding the moral order just as a citadel preserves the existence of a city—any breach endangers the entire structure. There is no doubt that monotheism occupies this central place among moral virtues. It is the highest and most fundamental expression of justice, as affirmed by the Qur'ān. For this reason, associating partners with God is described as a grave injustice and explicitly declared an unforgivable crime. As a result, people will be forsaken, condemned and consigned to hell.

What is *shirk* (polytheism)? If anyone is made into a deity alongside God, the Qur'ān refers to this—within its own terminology—as *shirk*. It means believing that someone proceeds from the essence *(dhāt)* of God, or that God proceeds through the essence of another. It also includes the idea that someone has a share in creation *(khalq)* or in the affairs of governance *(tadbīr al-umūr)*. In doing so, such a person is, in one way or another, made a coequal with God.

The first case is illustrated by the beliefs of Christians concerning Jesus (PBUH), Lady Mary, and the angels, as well as those of the polytheists of Arabia. The Sufi doctrine of *waḥdat al-wujūd* ("Unity of Being") also falls into this category.

The second case is illustrated by the beliefs of Hindus regarding *Brahma, Vishnu, and Shiva,* and of Muslims regarding figures such as *Ghawth, Quṭb, 'Abdāl, Dātā, and Gharīb Nawāz*. Beliefs in the influence of evil spirits, celestial bodies, and devils are likewise to be considered part of this category.

The following section contains detailed commandments related to this subject.

1. Worship of God

The first commandment is that if there is no deity except God, then worship must be exclusively for Him. As previously explained, the essence of worship is humility and submission, which initially manifests as reverence. Then, in view of human practical existence, this adoration takes the form of obedience. The manifestations of adoration include glorification and praise, supplication, bowing and prostration, making vows, presenting offerings and sacrifices, and secluding oneself for devotion. In the form of obedience, a person acknowledges someone's authority as an independent legislator and submits to their commands. The decision of God, the Lord of the Worlds, is that none of these acts—whether adoration in its various forms or obedience in recognition of divine authority—can be directed toward anyone but Him. Therefore, if a person glorifies, supplicates to, bows or prostrates before someone other than God, presents vows, offerings, or sacrifices to them, secludes themselves for their sake, or obeys them while acknowledging their divine authority, it amounts to a rejection of God Almighty's decree.

2. Kindness to Parents

The second commandment is to treat parents with kindness. This teaching has been given in all the divine scriptures. There is no doubt that among humans, the most paramount right belongs to the parents. Therefore, immediately after the command to worship God, fulfilling the rights of parents has been emphasized. The reason for this is that parents are the means through which a person comes into existence and is nurtured. The advice of God Almighty regarding the mother and the father is that, after showing gratitude to the Lord, a person should be most grateful to them.

This gratitude is not just expressed through words. There are essential requirements for it detailed in the Qurʾān.

i. The first point stated is that one should behave towards their parents in a way that they respect them both outwardly and inwardly, do not harbor any resentment towards them in their heart, do not utter any word of disrespect in their presence, but rather adopt an attitude of gentleness, love, nobility, and virtuous conduct. They should listen to their parents and provide comfort and consolation in their old age.

ii. The second point is that children should always show humility and obedience toward their parents, no matter the situation—and this obedience should be rooted in genuine love and compassion. Just as parents protect their children, like birds sheltering their young under their wings, children should care for their aging parents with the same protective love and devotion. This is the only way to truly honor the love and care parents have given. Without this heartfelt attitude, fulfilling their right is simply not possible.

iii. The third point is that, along with showing kindness and obedience, children should continuously pray for their parents, asking the Lord: just as they nurtured us with love and tenderness in our childhood, may He now envelop them in His mercy in their old age. This prayer is not only the rightful due of the parents but also a powerful reminder of the sacred responsibilities placed upon the offspring. Moreover, it nurtures the spirit of love that God Almighty has commanded us to uphold in honoring and serving our parents.

Beyond parents, this attitude should be extended in widening circles—to relatives, orphans, the needy, neighbors, travelers, and subordinates—as God Almighty has advised.

3. Spending in the Way of God

The third commandment is to spend in the way of God. This means that whatever blessings God Almighty has granted a person, just as they spend on themselves—after fulfilling their personal and business needs—they should also spend on other human beings. The Qur'ān clearly states that to live in this world as a true servant of God, two things are essential:

i. First, that a person establishes a proper relationship with the Creator.

ii. Second, that they build a rightful connection with His creation.

The first is achieved through prayer, which is the foremost

expression of love for God Almighty; the second, through spending, which is the foremost expression of love for His creation. And the reward for this too is the love of God, for whatever a person spends is, in reality, being stored for the Hereafter. As the words of Prophet Jesus (PBUH) states:

> *"For where your treasure is, there your heart will be also."*
>
> *(Matthew, 6:19-21).*

This spending is the right of relatives, orphans, and the needy, which is obligatory to fulfill. Negligence in this can make a person a criminal in the eyes of God Almighty for usurping the rights of others. The Qurʾān has clearly stated at one place that if a person ignores these rights and accumulates wealth, then it is a hoarded wealth *(Kanz)*, and its punishment is the fire of hell, from which every believer should seek refuge from their Lord.

The motivation to spend like this is granted to those who adopt a moderate attitude in their expenses and consider the sustenance granted by God Almighty not as the result of their own planning or wisdom but as a blessing from God. Additionally, two more points are made:

i. One is that squandering wealth frivolously is not permissible. It is a blessing from God, and the correct attitude toward it is that a person should spend on their legitimate needs with moderation and a sense of sufficiency, and regard whatever is saved as a trust of the rightful owners, to be discharged with utmost care.

This is because a person who does not adopt a balanced and equitable attitude in fulfilling their needs becomes excessively occupied with their own desires and neglects the rights of others. God says that those who squander their wealth in this manner are brothers of the devils, and the devil is ever ungrateful to his Lord. He deceives them and engages them in spending on deeds that, instead of gaining God's satisfaction, earn His displeasure.

The correct point of moderation is explained in this manner: a person should neither keep their hands completely tied nor leave them completely open, lest they find themselves deprived and reproached at the time of need. Rather, they should spend with moderation and always save a portion so that they are able to fulfill both their own rights and the rights of others in a timely manner.

ii. The second point is that the scarcity or abundance of sustenance lies entirely in the wisdom and will of God Almighty. A person's duty is only to make full effort in seeking its means. Those who fail to understand this reality—far from spending on others—often become so overwhelmed by the fear of poverty that they even commit the heartless act of killing their own children. This refers especially to the cruel practice in pre-Islamic Arabia of burying infant girls alive, based on the belief that, since a woman does not earn, raising her would be a financial burden. But God says: Do not kill them; We provide sustenance for them and for you. Rest assured, God is fully aware of His servants' conditions and is ever watchful over them.

4. Chastity and Virtue

The fourth commandment is that no one should even approach adultery. The reason given is that it is a flagrant indecency and a most evil path. This means that its immorality and depravity are self-evident and need no further argument or proof.

Human nature has always regarded it as a grave sin and a serious crime—and will continue to do so unless it becomes completely corrupted.

It is an undeniable truth about human beings that the institution of family is as essential to them as air and water. This institution can only be formed and sustained through proper natural emotions, which are nurtured when the bond between spouses is one of ongoing companionship. If this element is absent, society risks becoming a herd of beings stripped of both natural and spiritual sentiment—conditions under which a healthy civilization can never be built.

It is because of the repugnance of this act that God Almighty did not merely say, "Do not commit adultery," but rather commanded, "Do not even go near it." It means to stay away from all those things that provoke adultery, tempt toward it, and lead to it. The etiquette of the interaction between men and women mentioned in the Qurʾān are set to protect humans from these very things. In summary, both men and women should protect their gazes as much as possible and cover the areas of their bodies that can incite temptation, and they should not say anything that could provoke the sexual feelings of the other. The reason is that when Satan wishes to make adultery common in a society, he generally starts with these very things. It is known from the Qurʾān that Adam and Eve were also attacked by Satan through this path. God Almighty has considered the act of spreading adultery and creating temptations for it as a great crime for this reason.

5. The Sanctity of Human Life

The fifth commandment is that no one should take the life of another. This highlights the sanctity that human life has always held in both religion and morality. The Qur'ān informs us that the same command was given to the Children of Israel, and that God Almighty had decreed for them that killing a single person is, in essence, like killing all of humanity.

Additionally, the Qur'ān makes it clear that those who commit this crime are accountable not only to God Almighty but also to the relatives of the victim, who have been granted full authority in this matter. Therefore, no court in the world has the right to grant leniency to the murderer without the consent of the victim's family. It is the court's duty to support them if they demand retribution *(Qiṣāṣ)* and to ensure that their wishes are carried out fully and accurately.

6. Embezzling the Property of Orphans

The sixth commandment is that no wrongful act should be committed with the property of orphans. The words of this commandment are the same as those that came to prevent adultery. That is, do not even approach an orphan's property except with the intent of enhancing their well-being. This means that only those dealings with an orphan's property are permitted, which are aimed at its protection and growth, and only until the orphan reaches maturity and is capable of managing their own wealth

7. Adherence to Agreements

The seventh commandment is to fulfill any agreement made in all circumstances. God says that you will be questioned about it. This commandment has also appeared at other places in the Qur'ān with the same emphasis. The most important directive regarding *Jihād* and warfare in the Qur'ān is the strict adherence to agreements. When the Prophet Muhammad (PBUH) and his companions were instructed to end all treaties with the polytheists of Arabia and take a final stand, it was also made clear that any agreement set for a specific duration must be honored until its term expires. Furthermore, the Qur'ān clarifies that even if a treaty partner is oppressing Muslims, helping them cannot involve violating the terms of the agreement.

8. Honesty in Weight and Measure

The eighth commandment is to ensure honesty in measurement and weight in trade. God Almighty has commanded that just as He created the heavens and the earth with balance; humans must uphold justice within their own spheres by measuring accurately and using proper scales. This is a critical commandment rooted in the very balance of justice upon which the world is founded. Anyone who deviates from this principle disrupts the concept of justice and undermines the belief that God is Just. Such actions inevitably lead to the breakdown of the economic and social systems, causing the very foundations of civilization to crumble.

The issue of adulteration falls under this commandment as well. Selling diluted milk, sand-mixed sugar, or barley-mixed wheat is a similar transgression. Even when the correct quantity is given, the buyer does not receive the pure product they paid for. This is, in essence, a violation of others' rights, which carries negative consequences in both this world and the hereafter. Therefore, it is commanded: give full measure when you measure and weigh with an accurate scale, as this is better and leads to a favorable outcome.

9. Avoiding Superstitions

The ninth commandment is that one should not follow anything without true knowledge. The Qur'ān cautions against treating this matter lightly, as every person's hearing, sight, heart, and mind will be held accountable before God one day. This means it is not permissible for a Muslim to suspect or accuse anyone without proper investigation, to act against someone based on mere suspicions, to spread rumors, or to hold beliefs about the essence, attributes, and decrees of their Lord based on doubts, superstitions, or baseless conjectures.

10. Pride and Arrogance

The tenth commandment is that no one should walk upon God's earth with arrogance, as this is the manner of the haughty and the prideful. It is stated that no matter how forcefully you tread, you cannot split the earth, and no matter how high you hold your head, you cannot match the height of the mountains.

Such a way of walking, clearly, reflects a person's inner state. Things like wealth, power, elegance, knowledge, and strength—all of which can foster arrogance—manifest outwardly in a particular manner of walking, revealing a heart that lacks the awareness of servitude and is oblivious to the greatness of God. In contrast, a heart filled with the consciousness of servitude and reverence for God's greatness belongs to those marked by humility and modesty. They walk with their heads bowed, free from strutting or boasting.

It should also be made clear that a person's pride and arrogance are not only evident in their walk, but also in their speech, demeanor, attire, how they carry themselves in company, and how they conduct their affairs—all of it reflects their inner state. Accordingly, all such things that show off wealth or relate to bragging, taking undue advantage, intimidating others, or adopting the manners of bullies should be considered forbidden. Even in growing beards, mustaches, and wearing clothes, no arrogant demeanor should be adopted.

Moreover, this mindset of self-pride leads to major sins. Indeed, it is a reality that denying the truth purposely, considering oneself superior based on race or lineage, mocking others, taunting them, calling them by bad epithets, and slandering them behind their backs are sins driven by this very pride and arrogance. God Almighty has strictly forbidden all these things.

Just as the commandments of the Torah, these are the Ten Commandments of the Qurʾān. All moralities stem from these ten commandments. The sins that God Almighty has referred to as major sins and acts of indecency originate from violating these commandments. The Qurʾān is very clear on this matter that people may have to bear the punishment for these violations on the Day of Judgment. Therefore, it is necessary for every Muslim to be cautious in this matter.

For this purpose, the following three points must be kept in mind:

i.   Firstly, if any of these commandments is violated inadvertently, then God will not hold one accountable. His rule is that if something happens unintentionally—even if it appears to be a forbidden act—but there is, in reality, no intention of committing it, He will not hold the person accountable.

ii. Secondly, if a person keeps themselves from violating these commandments, then the reward for this is that God Almighty will forgive their minor sins with His boundless mercy. Otherwise, both small and big sins will be recorded in their book of deeds, and they will have to account for them.

iii. Thirdly, if a person, overwhelmed by emotion, ends up violating any of these commandments, they must repent and correct their behavior without delay. It is essential that repentance be made as soon as possible. God Almighty has clearly stated in the Qur'ān that only those people have a right to repentance who fall into sin due to emotional weakness and then repent immediately. On the other hand, God does not accept the repentance of two types of people: those who remain immersed in sin throughout their lives and, upon seeing death approach, begin uttering words of repentance; and those who knowingly reject the truth and persist in denial until the very end.

These are the two conditions the Qur'ān outlines regarding the acceptance and rejection of repentance. Beyond these, the Qur'ān is silent on one remaining situation: when a person neither repents immediately after sinning nor delays it until death is near. This silence leaves room for both hope and fear, indicating that such cases lie between the two extremes. For such individuals, there remains the possibility of intercession.

Elegance and Perfection

When a person's moral character reaches perfection—both in relation to the Creator and to fellow human beings—it naturally gives rise to certain qualities, or, as the Qur'ān indicates, it should give rise to them. God lists them in a single place in the Qur'ān—ten qualities to which nothing is added anywhere else in the text. These ten qualities represent the elegance and perfection *(Jamal o Kamal)* of religion, and believers are called upon to strive for and fully embody them.

The traits are as follows:

1. **Islam**: The first trait is Islam. When mentioned in connection with faith, as it is here, it refers to the outward dimension of religion—that is, the guidance related to a person's words, deeds, and physical faculties. When a person's tongue speaks or remains silent in obedience to the command of God and His Messenger; when their eyes look or turn away in accordance with divine instruction; when their ears are eager to listen or to refrain based on God's guidance; when their hands act or hold back as directed; and when their feet move or halt at His command—this is what is meant by Islam. The Qur'ān presents the Prophets as the most perfect examples of this submission. Therefore, to attain this level of submission and contentment, individuals are urged to follow the personalities whom God has sent as His messengers.

2. **Faith:** The second trait is faith. It represents the inner dimension of religion, defined here as the certainty that arises from a true understanding of God and His promises. One who believes in God with such conviction that they surrender their heart and mind to Him with the utmost submission and contentment is, in Qur'ānic terminology, a believer. Faith purifies the heart, enlightens the intellect, and refines intentions. It is this faith that simultaneously influences both knowledge and action, and permeates a person's entire being. It grows through the remembrance of God, the recitation of His verses, and by reflecting on His signs within oneself and throughout

the universe. The Qur'ān calls upon those with faith to cherish nothing in the world more than God and His Messenger.

3. **Devotion** *(Qunoot)*: The third trait is devotion—a state of the heart that keeps a person in constant obedience to their Lord with complete sincerity and focus. It is the most prominent expression of the servant's relationship with the Master—a relationship that resides in the innermost depths of a believer's being. Therefore, the truly devoted *(Qānitīn)* are those who remain perpetually in a state of servitude. Whether in sorrow or pain, joy or passion, or even moments of intense pleasure, they never become defiant toward their Creator. The force of lust, the onslaught of emotions, and the crowding of countless desires never cause them to lose reverence before God. Their heart becomes the throne of God's presence, and they perceive His law as a command issued in divine audience—where even the thought of disobedience cannot arise, just as one standing in the royal court dares not defy the king. Upon reflection, this is the very state that the entire universe and all of its creatures are expressing— through the existential expression of their constant and uninterrupted submission.

4. **Truthfulness:** The fourth trait is truthfulness, which represents consistency and alignment between one's words, actions, and intentions. When a person consistently speaks the truth, when there is no contradiction between what they say and what they do, and when they fulfill every commitment they make, this reflects truthfulness in both word and deed. However, truthfulness is

not complete without sincerity of intention. The Qur'ān describes the opposite of this consistency as hypocrisy and defines its presence as sincerity—emphasizing that, in God's eyes, the real value of any deed lies in the intention formed in the heart. Therefore, the highest level of truthfulness is reached when speech, action, and intention are in perfect harmony.

5. **Patience:** The fifth trait is patience. In its initial sense, patience means restraining oneself from agitation and restlessness. Over time, it has come to embody perseverance, steadfastness, and unwavering commitment in the face of difficulties and trials. Patience is not a form of humiliation or degradation born of helplessness and despair; rather, it is a source of resolve and courage, and the foundation of moral refinement and behavioral excellence. It empowers a person to embrace life's challenges willingly, without complaint or bitterness—recognizing them as coming from God and submitting to them as such. Patience enables one to remain undisturbed by delays in outcomes, to suppress the urge for revenge against those who cause harm, and to stand firm in defense of the truth—even in the face of death. It involves maintaining self-control in both sorrow and joy, and remaining committed to what is recognized as a lifelong duty or calling.

This quality strengthens the bond between the servant and the Lord, often referred to as trust in God—placing complete reliance on Him in all situations. The phrase, "Indeed, we belong to God, and indeed to Him we will return," encapsulates the spirit of delegation and surrender. The Qur'ān promises that those who live by this conviction and depart from this world with it will be granted God's special mercy and grace.

6. **Reverent Humility** *(Khushū)*: The sixth thing is Reverent humility. It is the humility, submission, and meekness produced inside a person by a correct understanding of God's awe and His grandeur and majesty. The Qur'ān describes it as reverent humility & devout attentiveness *(Khushū)*. It is a condition of the heart that makes one bow before God and also generates feelings of mercy and compassion towards other human beings. In the first case, the best expression of it is in prayer, especially the night prayers, when a believer, isolated from all worldly affairs, whispers to his Lord and fills his moments of solitude with His remembrance and gratitude.

In the second case, this condition affects the entire personality of a believer, making him a source of mercy for his family, a sea of compassion for his friends, neighbors, and acquaintances, and a fountain of guidance for his society. Such patient and kind-hearted people give rise to a civilization that becomes God's paradise on earth and the focal point of every sound-natured person's aspirations and desires.

7. **Charity**: The seventh trait is charity. One level of giving in the way of God is for a person to consistently fulfill the obligatory charity *(Zakāt)* from their wealth. A second, higher level is to regard whatever exceeds one's personal and business needs as a right of others, and to fulfill this responsibility generously whenever a need arises. The third and highest level is to suppress one's own desires and make personal sacrifices to meet the needs of others.

While the phrase "those who give charity" can include all these levels, when described as a moral trait, it specifically refers to this highest degree of generosity—one who is open-handed and does not miss any opportunity to give in the path of God. In relation to others, this quality reflects the same reverent humility mentioned earlier. This is why the Qurʾān often pairs prayer and charity together, emphasizing their deep interconnectedness.

8. **Fasting:** The eighth trait is fasting, a unique act of worship that fosters self-restraint and cultivates patience. The purpose of fasting, as stated in the Qurʾān, is to develop God-consciousness *(Taqwā)*. Therefore, when describing qualities, "those who fast" refers to individuals who are so committed to *Taqwā* that they frequently observe fasts. This implies that they actively avoid wrongdoing, refrain from indecencies, and embody the highest moral virtues in their lives.

9. **Guarding Private Parts:** The ninth trait is guarding the private parts—referring to those who protect their sexual organs from exposure or misuse. This is a direct outcome of self-restraint and God-consciousness *(Taqwā)*. In several places, the Qurʾān uses this phrase to describe those who avoid nudity, indecent exposure, and acts of lewdness. It means they safeguard their chastity and personal dignity to the highest degree. As such, except in circumstances permitted by God, they do not expose their private parts to anyone — neither in private nor public. Moreover, they avoid wearing clothing that highlights or draws attention to parts of the body naturally associated with sexual attraction. This standard of avoiding

lewdness forms the moral foundation of a society where modesty is honored, and both men and women strive not to expose their bodies, but to cover them with dignity and intentional care.

10. **Abundant Remembrance:** The tenth trait is abundant remembrance, or the continuous remembrance of God. When a faithful servant's heart is deeply anchored in the thought of their Lord, they do not limit worship to prescribed times but keep their tongue constantly engaged in the remembrance of God. They say *"Glory be to God" (subḥān Allāh)* upon witnessing any sign of God, begin every task with *"In the name of God" (bismi Allāh)*, express gratitude by saying *"Praise be to God" (al-ḥamdu li-llāh)* when receiving blessings, and affirm intentions with *"If God wills" (in shāʾ Allāh)* and *"As God has willed" (mā shāʾ Allāh)*. They seek God's help in all affairs, call upon His mercy in affliction, and turn to Him in hardship. They sleep and wake up with His name on their lips. In every moment and matter, their tongue is engaged in God's remembrance. This devotion extends to prayers, fasting, Qurʾān recitation, charitable giving, avoidance of evil, and seeking forgiveness immediately after any misstep.

This remembrance also takes the form of contemplation. Observing God's creation—the diversity of creatures, the wonders of human intellect, the vast oceans, flowing rivers, lush greenery, rainfall, the rotation of day and night, the interactions of wind and clouds, the magnificent construction of the earth and skies—each element serves a purpose, reflecting wisdom and benefit. Signs of God are present within oneself and throughout the universe, constantly revealing themselves in new forms.

When a faithful servant reflects upon these divine signs, their heart and mind become absorbed in the remembrance of God. Filled with awe, they proclaim: Lord, You have not created this magnificent universe without purpose. It does not befit Your knowledge and wisdom to do anything in vain. I am certain that this vibrant and beautiful world will one day come to an end—and that end will be the Day of Recompense. On that Day, those who regarded this world as the idle amusement of a playful being—created without seriousness or purpose—will face punishment and disgrace. I seek refuge in You from such an end.

PART 2

THE LAW

(Al-Kitāb)

THE LAW OF WORSHIP

The purpose of religion is purification. The way to reach its ultimate perfection is through the establishment of the relationship between servant and God in the proper way. The stronger this relationship is, the more a person progresses in the purity of their knowledge and actions. Love, fear, sincerity, loyalty, and feelings of gratitude and acknowledgment for God Almighty's boundless blessings and infinite favors are the inner manifestations of this relationship. This relationship typically manifests in a person's daily life in three forms:

1. worship,
2. obedience, and
3. zeal and support.

The religion brought by the Prophets has prescribed specific acts of worship to remind us of our relationship with God.

Prayer and almsgiving *(Zakāt)* are acts of worship; fasting and seclusion in a mosque are expressions of obedience; and Ḥajj and ʿUmra are symbolic demonstrations of zeal and allegiance to the Almighty. The essence of sacrifice reflects the same reality.

Prayer *(Ṣalāh)*

Among these, the most important act of worship is prayer. The essence of religion, if considered carefully, is the recognition of God and standing before Him with feelings of fear and love, with humility and submission. The most prominent manifestation of this essence is worship. Praises and glorifications of God, supplication, and prostration are the practical forms of this worship. Prayer encompasses all these aspects with utmost balance.

The significance of this act of worship in religion is extraordinary. Just as monotheism holds the highest status in the domain of faith, prayer holds the same status in the domain of deeds. It has been made obligatory to keep the remembrance of God alive. The Qurʾān informs us that the recognition of God and the feelings of love and gratitude that arise—or should arise—through reflecting on God's signs are manifested in the form of prayer.

Prayer is the pillar of Islam, a condition for a person to be considered a Muslim in both this world and the hereafter, a means of steadfastness in faith, a remover of distress, an eraser of sins, a mark of the call to truth, a foundation for commitment to the path of righteousness, the nature of the universe, and true life itself.

When the recognition of God, along with His remembrance

and contemplation, and the sense of His closeness reach their highest point, they manifest as prayer. The consensus of sages around the world is that true life is the life of the heart, and the life of the heart is found in this recognition, remembrance, contemplation, and feeling of closeness to God. This life is both attained and sustained through prayer.

The History of Prayer

Its history is as ancient as religion itself. The concept of prayer has been present in all religions, and its rituals and timings have been more or less determined. The hymns of Hindus, chants of Zoroastrians, prayers of Christians, and psalms of Jews are all memorials of this.

The Qurʾān has told us that all of God's Prophets taught it. It holds the most prominent status in the religion of Prophet Abraham (PBUH), which the Prophet Muhammad (PBUH) was sent to revive. When the Qurʾān commanded it, it was not something unfamiliar to the people. They were already well aware of its ritual manners, conditions, and the actions and recitations it involved.

Therefore, there was no need for the Qurʾān to detail it. As it was performed as a tradition of the religion of Abraham (PBUH), the Prophet Muhammad (PBUH), with some amendments as commanded by the Qurʾān, continued it for his followers, and generation after generation, they have been performing it in the same manner.

Conditions for Prayer

The prerequisites for prayer are:

1. the person performing it should not be intoxicated,

2. if a woman, she should not be in a state of menstruation or postnatal bleeding,

3. should have performed ablution *(Wuḍū)*, and if after menstruation, postnatal bleeding, or major ritual impurity *(Janāba)*, should have taken a full ritual bath *(Ghusl)*

4. In case of travel, illness, or scarcity of water, if both ablution and bathing become difficult, then one should perform dry ablution *(Tayammum)*,

5. Should stand facing *Qibla*,

The procedure for ablution is to first wash the face, then wash the arms up to the elbows, wipe the entire head, and then wash the feet.

Once ablution is performed, it remains valid until a nullifying action occurs. Hence, the requirement for ablution applies only when one's previous ablution is no longer valid—unless, of course, one chooses to perform a fresh ablution simply to feel spiritually refreshed.

The nullifiers include:

1. Urination.

2. Defecation.

3. Passing of gas, whether audible or silent.

4. Emission of pre-ejaculatory fluid or urethral discharge.

In circumstances where water is unavailable or its use is genuinely difficult—due to travel, illness, or scarcity—God Almighty has permitted the performance of dry ablution. This is done by placing the hands on a clean surface and then wiping the face and hands with the palms, serving as a substitute for both ablution and ritual bathing. *Tayammum* can be performed if any nullifiers of ablution occur, and after sexual intercourse, *tayammum* can be used as a substitute for full-body ritual bath *(Ghusl al-janāba)*. Additionally, even if water is available during illness or travel, *tayammum* remains an option.

While *tayammum* might not appear to provide actual physical purification, it maintains the symbolic essence of purification. The *Sharīʿah* generally considers that if fulfilling a command in its original form is impossible or overly challenging, a symbolic alternative is prescribed to preserve its remembrance. This approach ensures that, as soon as circumstances return to normal, a person's natural inclination is to return to the original practice.

Practices of Prayer:

The prescribed acts for prayer are as follows:

1. Prayer begins with raising the hands upward *(Rafʿ al-Yadayn)*.
2. Standing *(Qiyām)*
3. Then comes bowing *(Rukūʿ)*.
4. This is followed by standing upright again *(Qawma)*.
5. Next are two successive prostrations *(Sujūd)*.
6. In every second and final unit *(Rakʿā)* of prayer, the person praying sits briefly *(Qaʿda)*.
7. When concluding the prayer, one turns their face to the sides while seated to formally end the prayer.

Invocations in Prayer

The invocations *(adhkār)* in prayer are as follows:

1. At the start of prayer, say *"Allāhu akbar"*,
2. Recite Sūrat al-Fātiḥah (the first chapter of the Qurʾān)

during standing *(qiyām)*, then recite any other part of the Qur'ān as convenient.

3. Say *"Allāhu akbar"* while going into bowing *(rukū')*.

4. Upon rising from bowing say *"Sami'a Allāhu liman ḥamidahu"*

5. Say *"Allāhu akbar"* while going into prostration *(Sujūd)* and rising from it, and while moving from sitting position to standing.

6. To conclude the prayer, say *"al-salāmu 'alaykum wa raḥmat Allāh."*

Allāhu akbar ("God is the Greatest"), *Sami'a Allāhu liman ḥami-dahu* ("God hears the one who praises Him"), and *al-salāmu 'alaykum wa raḥmat Allāh* ("Peace and mercy of God be upon you") must always be said aloud by the prayer leader *(imām)*.

The Qur'ān is recited aloud by the *Imām* in the first two units of the Sunset (Maghrib) prayer and the Night ('Ishā') prayer. Recitation is also done aloud in the Dawn (Fajr) prayer, the Friday (Jum'a) prayer, and the Festival *('Īd)* prayers.

Recitation is done silently in the third unit *(Rak'ā)* of the Sunset (Maghrib) prayer, the third and fourth units of the Night ('Ishā') prayer, and in all four units *(Rak'āt)* of the Noon (Ẓuhr) and Afternoon ('Aṣr) prayers.

According to *Sharī'ah*, these are the only mandatory pre-scribed remembrances, and they are specifically required to be in Arabic. Apart from these, the person praying can include any supplication or glorification in any language within their prayer.

Times of Prayer

Every Muslim is required to perform five daily prayers at spe-cific times throughout the day and night:

1. Dawn (Fajr): Begins when the first white light appears in the sky, separating from the darkness, and lasts until sunrise.

2. Noon (Ẓuhr): Begins when the sun passes its highest point (zenith) and continues until the beginning of ʿAṣr.

3. Afternoon (ʿAṣr): Begins when the sun enters the field of vision—that is, when its angle lowers and it starts casting longer shadows—and continues until sunset.

4. Sunset (Maghrib): Begins immediately after sunset and lasts until the onset of ʿIshāʾ.

5. Night (ʿIshāʾ): Begins when the red twilight disappears from the sky and continues until the middle of the night.

Since sunrise and sunset were times of worship in some earlier traditions, prayer is prohibited during these periods. The timing of these prayers has remained constant in the religion of all the Prophets.

Units of Prayer

The prescribed units *(Rakʿāt)* for prayer are as follows:

1. Fajr: 2,

2. Ẓuhr: 4,

3. ʿAṣr: 4,

4. Maghrib: 3,

5. ʿIshāʾ: 4.

These are the obligatory units *(Rakʿāt)* of prayer—the very ones for which a person will be held accountable on the Day of Judgment if neglected. Therefore, except in cases where shortening *(Qaṣr)* is allowed, these must be performed without exception. All other prayers are voluntary *(Nafl)*; performing them brings reward, but there is no fear of accountability from Allāh for omitting them.

Concessions in Prayer

If the time for prayer arrives during danger, distress, chaos, or urgency, God has permitted offering the prayer while walking, riding, or in any feasible manner. It is evident that such prayers cannot be offered in congregation; facing the *Qibla* may not be required, and the physical actions of the prayer may not be performed in their usual prescribed manner.

In these situations, specifically during travel, the Qur'ān further permits the shortening of prayers, known as *Qasr.* According to the Sunna established by the Prophet Muhammad (PBUH), only prayers of four units are shortened to two units. There is no reduction in two or three-unit prayers; thus, as Fajr and Maghrib are performed in full even under such circumstances, as Fajr already consists of two units, and Maghrib is uniquely designed as an odd-numbered prayer to complete the daily total of *Rak'āt* on an odd count, their format remains unchanged.

From this permission to shorten prayers, it is also inferred that combining prayers during travel is allowed. Thus, Ẓuhr and ʿAṣr, as well as Maghrib and ʿIshā', may be performed together.

Congregational Prayer

Although prayers may be performed individually, it is preferable to offer them in congregation—and, if possible, in a mosque. When the Prophet Muhammad (PBUH) arrived in Yathrib, his first act was to build a mosque, thereby establishing the tradition of constructing mosques in every community and neighborhood. Attending the mosque and making arrangements for congregational prayer is highly virtuous. While women are exempt, no Muslim man should miss it without a valid excuse. The method for establishing congregational prayer is as follows:

1. The call to prayer, known as *Ādhān*, is made before the prayer to gather people for the congregation. The words of the *Ādhān*, as established by the Prophet Muhammad (PBUH), are as follows:

   a. *Allāhu akbar* – "God is the Greatest"

   b. *Ashhadu an lā ilāha illā llāh* – "I bear witness that there is no deity but God"

   c. *Ashhadu Anna Muḥammadan Rasūl Allāh* – "I bear witness that Muhammad (PBUH) is the Messenger of God"

   d. *Ḥayya ʿala ṣ-ṣalāh* – "Come to the prayer"

   e. *Ḥayya ʿala -falāḥ* – "Come to success"

   f. *Allāhu akbar* – "God is the Greatest"

   g. *Lā ilāha illā llāh* – "There is no deity but God"

2. If there is only one follower, he will stand to the right of the *Imām*; if more, the *Imām* will stand in front and they will form rows behind him.

3. To initiate the prayer, *Iqāma* will be said, repeating the words of *Ādhān*. However, after "*Ḥayya ʿala l-falāḥ*", the one saying *Iqāma* will also say "*Qad qāmat aṣ-ṣalāh*" (Prayer has been established).

4. The words of *Ādhān* will be repeated more than once if necessary.

5. Similarly, the words of *Iqāma* can also be repeated if needed.

Mistakes in Prayer

For the acts and supplications prescribed in prayer, if a mistake occurs—or if there is doubt that one has occurred—the Sunna prescribes that the mistake should be corrected if possible. Whether or not it can be rectified, two additional prostrations should be performed at the end of the prayer.

Friday Prayer

On Fridays, Muslims are obligated to hold a special congregational prayer in place of the regular Ẓuhr prayer. The procedure for this prayer is as follows:

- The prayer consists of two units.
- Unlike the Ẓuhr prayer, loud recitation *(Qirā'at)* is performed in both units.
- Initial proclamation of God's greatness *(Takbīr)* is said for prayers
- Before the prayer, the prayer leader *(Imām)* delivers two sermons, both delivered while standing. Between the first and second sermon, the *Imām* sits briefly.
- The call to prayer *(Ādhān)* is given when the *Imām* arrives at the pulpit.
- Upon hearing the *Ādhān*, all Muslim men are required to cease their activities and attend the prayer, unless they have a valid excuse.

The responsibility for organizing this prayer rests with community leaders, and it is conducted only at designated locations, where either they or their representatives lead the prayer.

Festival (ʿĪd) Prayers

On the days of Festival of Breaking the Fast *(ʿĪd al-Fiṭr)* and

Festival of Sacrifice *(ʿĪd al-ʾAḍḥā)*, Muslims are also required to hold a congregational prayer after sunrise and before noon, similar to the Friday prayer. The procedure is as follows:

- This prayer consists of two units, with loud recitation in both.

- During the standing position, additional *Takbīrs* are proclaimed by the worshippers.

- Unlike regular prayers, there is no call to prayer *(Ādhān)* or *Iqāma*.

- After the prayer, the Imām will deliver two sermons for the purpose of advising and reminding the congregants. Both sermons are delivered while standing, with a brief sitting pause between them.

The address and conduct of this prayer follow the same pattern as the Friday prayer. It is authorized by community leaders and held at designated locations, where they or their appointed representatives lead the congregation.

Funeral Prayer

The funeral prayer for the deceased is also an obligatory act in the tradition of the Prophets.

After the body is washed and prepared, the prayer is performed as follows:

- The deceased is placed between the *Imām* and the direction of prayer *(Qibla)*, while the followers stand in rows behind the *Imām*.

- The prayer begins with raising the hands and saying *"Allāhu akbar."*

- Like the ʿĪd prayers, additional *Takbīrs* are recited,

- After the *Takbīrs* and supplications, the prayer concludes with *Salam* by turning the head to the side.

This concludes the essential acts of worship related to prayers that are required of Muslims. However, the Qur'ān encourages any voluntary acts of goodness, assuring that they are accepted by God, and advises seeking strength through patience and prayer in times of hardship. Therefore, in addition to the obligatory prayers, Muslims often observe voluntary prayers as well, with details provided in traditional teachings.

Mandatory Charity *(Zakāt)*

After prayer, this is the second most important act of worship. Among the various forms of worship that humans have historically practiced for their deities, one common act is to dedicate a portion of wealth, livestock, or produce as an offering. This is known as charity, offering, or sacrifice across different cultures.

In the religion of the Prophets, *Zakāt* fundamentally fulfills this purpose and is thus regarded as an act of worship. The Qur'ān often uses the term *Ṣadaqa* for *Zakāt*, emphasizing that it should be offered with a heart bowed in humility and burdened by the weight of one's moral duty. Traditionally, offerings would be handed to temple servants to support worshippers, but this practice has now ceased.

Muslims are now instructed to allocate this wealth for community needs under the guidance of their leaders, preserving its essence as a service devoted solely to God. When Muslims fulfill this duty, its acceptance is decreed by God Himself.

The History of *Zakāt*

Its history parallels that of prayer. According to the Qur'ān, the command of *Zakāt* has always been part of the laws given to previous Prophets. When Muslims were instructed to fulfill this obligation, it was not something unfamiliar; followers of the Abrahamic faith were already well-acquainted with its regulations. Thus, it was an established practice that Prophet Muhammad (PBUH), upon God's command and with necessary reforms, reinstated among Muslims.

The Purpose of *Zakāt*

Reflecting on its name reveals its purpose, which is growth and purification. Hence, *Zakāt* refers to the portion of wealth given to attain purity. This aligns with the broader objective of religion: to cleanse the soul from the ailments brought on by attachment to wealth, to bring blessings into one's wealth, and to enhance spiritual purity.

This obligatory act of giving is the minimum required from a Muslim as a contribution in the path of God. It draws the believer's heart closer to the Almighty and helps diminish the negligence that can arise from worldly pursuits.

The Law of *Zakāt*

The law of *Zakāt* is as follows:

With the exception of production, commerce, and business resources, personal use items, and capital below the minimum threshold *(Niṣāb)*, nothing is exempted from *Zakāt*. It will be imposed on all wealth, every type of livestock, and all kinds of produce, and it will be mandatorily collected from every Muslim citizen of the state every year.

Its rate is as follows:

- 2.5% annually on accumulated wealth.
- 10% on production if it results solely from capital or solely from labor. This is due each time production occurs.

- 5% on production if both capital and labor contribute. This is also due per production cycle.
- 20% if the gain is acquired without either capital or labor, as a pure gift or windfall from God.
- For livestock:
  a. Camel: from 5 to 24, one goat for every five camels; from 25 to 35, one yearling female camel, and if not available, then a two-year-old camel; from 36 to 45, one two-year-old female camel; from 46 to 60, one three-year-old female camel; from 61 to 75, one four-year-old female camel; from 76 to 90, two, two-year-old female camels; from 91 to 120, two, three-year-old female camels, and beyond 120, one two-year-old and one three-year-old female camel for every 40 and 50, respectively.
  b. Cows: one yearling calf for every 30, and one two-year-old calf for every 40.
  c. Goats: from 40 to 120, one goat; from 121 to 200, two goats; from 201 to 300, three goats, and beyond 300, one goat for every 100.

The expenditures of *Zakāt* as mentioned in the Qur'ān are detailed as follows:

  i. For the poor and needy,
  ii. As remuneration for state employees,
  iii. all political expenses in the interest of Islam and Muslims,
  iv. For the emancipation of individuals from all forms of slavery,
  v. to aid those burdened with loss, fines or debt,

vi. in the service of religion and

vii. for the welfare of the people, and

viii. for the aid of travelers and

ix. the construction of roads, bridges, inns, etc.

Ṣadaqat al-Fiṭr (The charity of breaking the fast) is also considered a form of *Zakāt*. It amounts to the value of a morning and evening meal and is obligatory on behalf of every Muslim in one's household, whether young or old. It is a compulsory charity given before the *Īd* prayer at the end of *Ramaḍān*.

Fasting

After prayer and *Zakāt* the third significant act of worship is *Fasting*. In Arabic, it's called *Ṣawm*, which means to stop or abstain from something. In Islamic terminology, this word is used specifically to denote abstaining from eating, drinking, and conjugal relations under certain conditions. In the Urdu language, this is referred to as *Roza*.

As human life unfolds in the realm of practical reality, the emotion of servitude to God Almighty—when fully integrated into this existence—demands not only worship but also obedience. Fasting stands as a symbolic manifestation of that obedience.

By this act, the servant expresses that, in response to their Lord's command and in pursuit of His pleasure, they willingly render some lawful things prohibited for themselves—becoming an embodiment of obedience and thereby asserting, through their very state, that nothing is greater than God and His command. If He declares any lawful thing to be prohibited, it is only fitting for the servant to submit unconditionally to His will.

This condition is a state of awareness and acknowledgment that affirms God's greatness and majesty; at its core, it is a genuine expression of gratitude. The Qur'ān describes fasting as a means of exalting God and showing gratitude to Him, designating the month of Ramaḍān for this purpose because it was during this month that guidance was revealed in the form of the Qur'ān. This guidance offers clear arguments for distinguishing between truth and falsehood, encouraging believers to exalt God and express their thankfulness.

The ultimate form of fasting involves imposing additional restrictions upon oneself and isolating from others for a few days to stay in the mosque and worship God as much as possible, known as I'tikāf. Though not obligatory like the fasts of Ramaḍān, it holds significant importance from the standpoint of self-purification. The special condition produced by the combination of fasting, prayer, and recitation of the Qur'ān, and the state of detachment and devotion to God that ensues, fulfills the true purpose of fasting at its highest level.

History of Fasting

Like prayer, the history of fasting is also very ancient. The Qur'ān states that fasting was made obligatory for Muslims just as it was for those before them, indicating that fasting has always been considered an important act of self-purification in all religions.

The Purpose of Fasting

The Qur'ān explains the purpose of fasting is to attain God-consciousness *(Taqwā)*. In Qur'ānic terms, God-consciousness means that a person should live their life within the limits set by God and always be wary in their heart of the consequences of crossing these limits, knowing that no one except God can save them.

The Law of Fasting

The law of fasting is as follows:

- Fasting means, with the intention *(Niyya)* of fasting, abstaining from eating, drinking, and conjugal relations solely for God's pleasure, from dawn until nightfall.

- Therefore, eating, drinking, and being with one's spouse is completely permissible during the nights of fasting.

- The month of Ramaḍān has been specifically designated for fasting, hence, anyone present in this month is obligated to observe fasts for its entirety.

- If someone cannot complete the fasts of Ramaḍān due to illness, travel, or other compelling reasons, it is obligatory for them to make up the missed days by fasting on other days.

- Fasting during menstruation and postnatal bleeding is prohibited, but these fasts must later be completed.

- *Iʿtikāf* – seclusion in a mosque for worship—is considered the highest expression of fasting. If God enables someone, they should withdraw from worldly distractions and remain in the mosque for as many days as possible during the month of fasting, leaving only for essential human needs.

  For a person in *Iʿtikāf*, there is no restriction on eating and drinking during the nights of fasting, but visiting one's spouse is not permitted. God has specifically prohibited this during *Iʿtikāf*.

Ḥajj and ʿUmra

Both these acts of worship are the pinnacle of worship in the Abrahamic faith. Their history begins with the proclamation made by Abraham, (PBUH), after constructing the Masjid al-Ḥarām, inviting people to come and offer their devotions to the Lord and renew the covenant of monotheism they have committed to.

The highest expression of devotion to God is for a person to stand ready to sacrifice everything—life and wealth—at His command, presenting themselves fully in His service. Ḥajj and ʿUmra are symbolic enactments of this very readiness. Both reflect the same underlying reality: ʿUmra serves as a concise version, while Ḥajj expands on it in such a way that the very purpose behind the sacrifice of life and wealth becomes vividly clear.

God Almighty has informed us that from the very beginning, Satan declared war against the divine plan that was set in motion with the creation of Adam. Since that day, the servants of God have been engaged in an ongoing struggle against this eternal enemy and his forces—a struggle that will continue until the Day of Judgment. This battle is the ultimate test of worldly life, upon which the eternal fate of humankind depends. The offering of one's life and wealth is, in essence, a contribution to this very struggle. Ḥajj embodies this fight against Satan in symbolic form. This representation includes:

- Upon hearing their Lord's call, God's servants detach themselves from worldly possessions, pleasures, and engagements. Then, chanting *"Labbayka, Labbayka"* (Here I am, here I am) they gather on the battlefield, settling in a valley just as warriors would.

- The next day, they move to an open field, seek forgiveness for their sins, and pray for victory in this battle through supplication and listening to their leader's sermon.

- In line with the allegory, prayers are shortened or combined, and after brief stops on the way, they return to their camps.

- Then follows the stoning of Satan, offering animal sacrifices, presenting oneself as a sacrifice to the Lord, shaving their heads, and performing the circuits around the primary house of worship and the sacrificial site.

- They continue to stone Satan for the next two or three days.

- In this regard, donning the *Iḥrām* symbolizes that a believer has relinquished worldly pleasures, activities, and desires, and has clothed themselves in two simple garments, presenting a nearly monk-like appearance before their Lord.

- The devotional chant *(Talbiyya)* is the response to the call made by our leader Abraham (PBUH), atop a rock after the reconstruction of the Sacred House of God. Now this call has reached every corner of the world, and God's servants, acknowledging His blessings and affirming His Oneness, respond to this call with the heartwarming chant, *"Labbayka, Allāhumma labbayka"* (Here I am, O Allāh, here I am)

- The circumambulation *(Ṭawāf)* represents the rounds of devotion. In the Abrahamic tradition, it has long been a practice that whatever is to be sacrificed, or whoever is dedicated for service in the sanctuary, is brought before the sanctuary or the place of sacrifice

- Touching the Black Stone symbolizes the renewal of the covenant. In this act, the devotee symbolically regards the stone as the hand of their Lord, places their hand upon it as if placing it in God's hand, and—adhering to the ancient tradition of covenant-making—kisses it to reaffirm their pledge: that by embracing Islam, they have surrendered their life and wealth in exchange for Paradise.

- The ritual walking between Ṣafā and Marwa *(Saʿy)* is a commemoration of Ishmael (PBUH) and signifies the path towards the place of sacrifice. Prophet Abraham (PBUH) had looked towards this sacrificial site standing on the mount of Ṣafā and then walked briskly towards Marwa to comply with the command. Thus, the *Saʿy* is also a ritual symbolizing the rounds of devotion around the sanctuary and the sacrificial site.

- Arafat serves as the alternative to the sanctuary where the warriors in this battle against Satan gather, seeking forgiveness for their sins and praying for success in this battle.

- Muzdalifa is a stop along the way where they spend the night and, before descending into the battlefield the next morning, engage once more in prayer and supplication.

- The Stoning of Satan *(Ramī)* serves as a profound symbol of rejecting and condemning Satan, reflecting the ongoing struggle against his influence. This act embodies the resolve of the faithful never to relent until Satan retreats. It acknowledges that Satan, as humanity's eternal adversary, persistently whispers temptations. However, steadfast resistance gradually diminishes his power. The ritual, performed over three days, begins on the first day by targeting the largest symbolic representation of Satan *(Jamrat al-ʿAqaba)*. On the following two days, the smaller ones are also targeted. This progression illustrates the diminishing influence of Satan as one perseveres in resisting him, emphasizing the journey of spiritual fortitude and victory over temptation.

- The sacrifice represents a symbolic offering in place of one's life, while shaving the head marks the fulfillment of the vow. Now, bearing this mark of obedience and lifelong servitude to their Lord, the believer may return home.

This showcases the extraordinary nature of the worship that has been made obligatory for every able Muslim at least once in their lifetime.

The Purpose of Ḥajj and ʿUmra

The purpose of Ḥajj and ʿUmra is the same as their essence:

- Acknowledging God Almighty's blessings,
- Affirming the belief in His Oneness,
- And reminding ourselves that by embracing Islam, we have dedicated ourselves to the service of our Lord.

These aspects and the deep penetration of this realization and conviction into our hearts and minds are what the Qurʾān refers to as the benefits of the stations of Ḥajj.

This purpose is beautifully clarified through the words prescribed for this act of worship. It becomes evident that these words have been chosen to highlight this purpose vividly and firmly embed it into our consciousness. Thus, after donning the *Iḥrām*, these words continuously resonate on the lips of every individual:

"Labbayka Allāhumma labbayk, labbayka lā sharīka laka labbayk. inna al-ḥamda wa al-niʿmata laka wa al-mulku, lā sharīka lak."

"Here I am, O God, here I am; here I am, You have no partner, here I am; surely all praise, grace, and sovereignty belong to You, You have no partner."

Days of Ḥajj and ʿUmra

There is no specified time for ʿUmra; it can be performed at any time throughout the year. As for Ḥajj, it is designated for the days from the 8th to the 13th of Dhū al-Ḥijja, and it can only be performed during these days.

Method of Ḥajj and ʿUmra

The prescribed method for Ḥajj and ʿUmra is as follows:

ʿUmra:

- Put on the *Iḥrām* with the intention of performing this act of worship.
- Those coming from outside should tie *Iḥrām* from their designated appointed boundary *(Mīqāt)*;
- Residents—whether they are locals of Mecca or staying temporarily—should put on the *Iḥrām* from a location outside the boundaries of the Ḥaram.
- and those living outside the boundary but within the *Mīqāt* should consider their residence as their *Mīqāt* and tie their *Iḥrām* from there and start reciting *Talbiyya*.
- The recitation of *Talbiyya* should be continued until reaching the Holy *Ka'bah*.
- Upon arrival, circumambulate the Ka'bah followed by performing *Saʿy* between *Ṣafā* and *Marwah*.

- If accompanied by sacrificial animals, perform their sacrifice.

- After the sacrifice, men should shave or trim their hair and women should cut a small portion of their hair from the end of their braid to undo the *Iḥrām*.

- *Iḥrām* signifies abstaining from sexual relations, not using any adornments or perfume, not cutting nails, not removing body hair, not cleansing oneself of dirt, even to the extent of not killing lice on one's body, not hunting, not wearing stitched clothing, keeping the head, face, and upper part of feet uncovered. Men should wrap one sheet around their waist and another over their shoulders,

- while women can wear stitched clothes and cover their head and feet but must keep their face and hands uncovered.

- *Mīqāt* are those designated places outside the boundary of Ḥaram set for pilgrims of Ḥajj and ʿUmra, beyond which they cannot proceed without *Iḥrām*.

    There are five designated Mīqāt points:

    1. Dhū al-Ḥulayfa (Abiyār ʿAlī) – for those coming from Madīnah.

    2. Yalamlam – for those coming from Yemen..

    3. Al-Juḥfa – for pilgrims arriving from the Levant (Syria, Jordan, Palestine, Lebanon) and Egypt.

    4. Qarn al-Manāzil – for pilgrims approaching from Najd.

    5. Dhāt ʿIrq – for pilgrims arriving from the northeast (e.g., Iraq and Persia).

- *Talbiyya* is the recitation of *"Labbayka Allāhumma labbayk, labbayka lā sharīka laka labbayk. inna al-ḥamda wa al-niʿmata laka wa al-mulku, lā sharīka lak"* which starts as soon as one ties *Iḥrām* and continues until reaching the Kaaba.

- The term *'Ṭawāf'* is used for the seven circumambulations, each starting and ending at the Black Stone[6], and includes kissing or touching it at the start of each round. If crowded, a gesture might suffice.

- *Saʿy* refers to the seven rounds between Ṣafā and Marwa. Like sacrifice, *Saʿy* is also performed voluntarily, and it's not a mandatory part of ʿUmra.

- The term *'Hady'* refers to animals specifically marked for sacrifice in the Ḥaram. They are distinguished by markings on their bodies and bands around their necks.

Ḥajj:

- Like ʿUmra, the first action for Ḥajj is to put on *Iḥrām* with the intention for Ḥajj.

- Those arriving from outside should enter into *Iḥrām* at their designated *Mīqāt* As for residents—whether permanent residents of Mecca, temporary visitors, or those living outside Mecca but within the boundaries of the *Mīqāt*—they should treat their place of residence as their *Mīqāt*, enter into *Iḥrām* there, and begin reciting the *Talbiyya*.

- On the 8th of Dhū al-Ḥijja, proceed to Minā and stay there.

---

6. *Hajr-e-Aswad* – This is a stone from the original structure of the House of God *(Baytullah)*, which has been placed in one of its corners as a symbol of the renewal of the covenant.

- On the morning of the 9th Dhū al-Ḥijja, set off for Arafat.

- Before the noon prayer, the *Imām* delivers the sermon of Ḥajj,

- then combine and shorten the Ẓuhr and ʿAṣr prayers.

- Engage in supplication, praise, and invocation until sunset.

- After sunset, move to Muzdalifa and combine and shorten the Maghrib and ʿIshāʾ prayers. Spend the night in Muzdalifa.

- After Fajr prayers, engage in supplication and invocation similar to Arafat, then head back to Minā.

- Upon reaching near the stone pillar, Jamrat al-ʿAqaba stop reciting *Talbiyya* and stone it with seven pebbles.

- If there are animals for *(Hady)* or if sacrifice for a vow or atonement is obligatory, perform the sacrifice.

- Then men should shave or trim their hair, and women should cut a small portion from the end of their braid, and take off the *Iḥrām*.

- Perform *Ṭawāf* of the *Kaʿbah*,

- all restrictions of *Iḥrām* will end with this. After that, if one wishes, the *Saʿy* between Ṣafā and *Marwah* may also be performed voluntarily, as a form of devotion.

- Return to Minā and stay for two or three days, stoning the three stone pillars, *Jamrat al-ʾŪlā, Jamrat al-Wusṭā,* and *Jamrat al-ʾAqabah* with seven pebbles each day.

The rituals of Ḥajj and ʿUmra have been the same since the time of Prophet Abraham (PBUH). The Qurʾān has not altered them but has clarified some related Islamic legal rulings, which are as follows:

1. Respecting the sanctities established by God for Ḥajj and 'Umrah is a demand of faith and must be upheld under all circumstances. However, if another party refuses to honor these sanctities, Muslims also have the right to take equal action because such sanctities can only be maintained mutually.

2. Despite this permission, Muslims cannot initiate any action on their own. These are the sanctities of God, and to breach them first is a grave sin that should not be committed under any circumstances.

3. The prohibition of hunting while in the state of *Iḥrām* applies exclusively to land animals. Fishing or consuming what others have hunted remains permissible. However, this exception should not be misused to circumvent the rule—hunting land animals is strictly forbidden. Anyone who knowingly violates this prohibition must offer atonement. There are three ways to atone for this act:

   i. Send an animal of the same species as the one hunted to the Ka'ba as a sacrifice.

   ii. Feed the needy with a meal equivalent in value to the hunted animal.

   iii. Fast for a number of days equal to the number of meals that would have been provided to the needy.

   If a substitute must be given in place of the sacrificial animals, or if offering them becomes impossible, then the matter of its value, the number of poor to be fed, or the number of fasts to be observed shall be determined by two upright men from among the Muslims. This ensures that those guilty of the offense have no opportunity to show leniency toward themselves.

4. The fourth directive is that if those traveling for Ḥajj or ʿUmra are prevented at some point and cannot proceed further, then they should send a sacrificial animal—whether a camel, cow, or goat—to Mecca for sacrifice. If that is not possible, they should perform the sacrifice at that very place, shave their heads, and come out of the state of *Iḥrām*. That will count as their Ḥajj or ʿUmrah.

In this matter, however, it must remain clear that whether the sacrifice is performed at such a place or in Mecca and Minā, shaving the head is not permissible before the sacrifice. The only exception is if a person is sick or has some ailment of the head and is compelled to shave before offering the sacrifice. In such a case, the Qurʾan grants permission to do so, but it must be compensated through fasting, giving charity, or offering another sacrifice. The number of days of fasting or the amount of charity for this expiation should be determined by the individual as he deems appropriate.

5. Pilgrims from outside who wish to perform Ḥajj and ʿUmra in a single journey can do so. They must first perform ʿUmra, undo their *Iḥrām*, and then enter into the state of *Iḥrām* again on the 8th of Dhū al-Ḥijja within Mecca to perform Ḥajj. This leniency is a concession by God due to the hardship of traveling twice. Therefore, they are to offer a sacrifice, which can be a camel, cow, or goat, whatever is available. If that's not possible, they must fast for ten days: three during Ḥajj and seven upon their return. This shows that God prefers separate journeys for Ḥajj and ʿUmra. Therefore, the Qurʾān clarifies

that this concession does not apply to those living near the Masjid al-Ḥarām.

6. The sixth directive is that pilgrims may depart from Minā on the 12th of Dhū al-Ḥijjah, or, if they choose, they may remain there until the 13ᵗʰ. God Almighty has made it clear that in either case there is no sin. What truly matters, therefore, is not the number of days spent in Minā, but that however long one stays, it is spent in the remembrance of God and in reverent fear of Him.

Sacrifice

In all religions of the world, sacrifice has been a central means of seeking closeness to God Almighty. Its essence is similar to that of *Zakāt* yet it is not primarily a sacrifice of wealth—but a symbolic offering of one's life, which is represented by the animal offered in its place.

The History of Sacrifice

Its history begins with Adam (PBUH). The Qur'ān narrates that when his two sons, (Abel and Cain), presented their offerings to God Almighty, one was accepted, while the other was not. The Bible clearly states that on this occasion, Abel had offered the sacrifice of some of the firstborn of his sheep and goats.

This practice, evidently, must have continued thereafter. Hence, its traces can be found in all religions. However, this act of worship certainly did not attain its full significance, eminence, and universality until after the sacrifice performed by Prophet Abraham (PBUH). When he was commanded to substitute his son with an animal, God Almighty stated that He had redeemed Ishmael with a great sacrifice. This meant that

Abraham's vow was accepted, and henceforth, people would commemorate this event through their own sacrifices. During Ḥajj, ʿUmra, and on the day of ʿĪd al-ʾAḍḥā, This is the sacrifice we meticulously perform as a supererogatory act of worship.

The Purpose of Sacrifice

The purpose is to express gratitude to God Almighty.When we symbolically sacrifice our lives through the offering of animals and present them before the Lord, we essentially express thanks for the guidance of submission and humility, which was demonstrated by Prophet Abraham (PBUH) through the sacrifice of his only son. The recitation of *Takbīr (Allāhu akbar: Allāh is the Greatest)* and *Tahlīl (Lā ilāha illā Allāh: There is no deity worthy of worship except Allāh)* during this occasion further reinforces this purpose, serving as a reminder of God's greatness and our devotion to Him.

Upon reflection, it represents the highest form of worship. As we and our animals face the *Qibla*—while the animal stands and is then laid in prostration—we proclaim, *"Bismillah, allāhu akbar"* (In the name of Allāh, Allāh is the Greatest). In dedicating the animal as an offering to God, we are, in reality, symbolically sacrificing ourselves to our Creator.

The Regulation of Sacrifice

The regulation is as follows:

- Sacrifice can be made of all types of livestock.
- The animal for sacrifice should be free from any blemishes and of appropriate age.
- The time for sacrifice begins after the ʿĪd al-ʾAḍḥā prayer on the 10th of Dhū al-Ḥijja. Its days are those designated

for stay in Minā after returning from Muzdalifa, traditionally known as the days of *Tashrīq*.

- Apart from the sacrifice, it is also a Sunna to proclaim *Takbīrs* — repeated declarations of "God is the Greatest" — after every congregational prayer during these days. The directive to recite the *Takbīrs* after prayers is general, without any specific wording prescribed by the *Sharī'ah*.

- The meat of the sacrifice can be consumed by the offerors themselves without hesitation and can also be fed to others.

THE LAW OF FAMILY
AND SOCIAL LIFE

The Creator has endowed man with the nature of a sociable creature. The reason for this is that man's creation is not such that his Maker fashions him somewhere in the heavens, sends him directly to the earth in the prime of youth, and then takes him back in the same youthful state without passing him through the stages of childhood and old age.

Contrary to this, his case is such that he comes into existence as a frail infant amidst layers of darkness. He opens his eyes in his mother's lap. He babbles, plays, eats and drinks through the care of others, and relies entirely on them to fulfill even his most basic needs. Initially, he crawls on the ground, then gradually manages to stand on his feet with great difficulty. Even after this, he requires support at every step. It is after going through several stages of childhood and adolescence that he reaches the age of fifteen or sixteen and becomes youthful. Even this period of youth does not last for more than twenty to thirty years.

Afterwards, signs of old age begin to appear, and after reaching the peak of knowledge and understanding, he again becomes dependent on others, much like a child, to complete the remaining days of his life.

The situation of man necessarily demands that he live a social life. From the very beginning of creation, this sociability has been present in him—in its complete and perfect form—both as a man and as a woman. They do not need to look outside themselves to realize this. When people enter this world, they bring with them all they need and establish their lives wherever they find themselves—be it in valleys, mountains, plains, or deserts.

History of mankind shows that with this very scheme in mind, when Prophet Adam (PBUH) came to this world as the first human, he was not sent alone, but God Almighty created a pair from his own kind for his companionship. Then, from them, many men and women were spread across the world, until the institution of family, tribe, and ultimately the state emerged, providing man with everything necessary for actualizing his hidden potentials.

It is these facts in view of which the permanent companionship of spouses has been adopted in the religion of the Prophets. Observing human life from childhood to old age, it becomes clear that this way of life is logical and natural considering his biological, psychological, and social needs.

This social nature has necessitated a comprehensive code

of conduct for its essential aspects, which was granted to the children of Adam through the Prophets.

This can be discussed under the following headings:

Marriage

The only legitimate way for men and women to fulfill their sexual needs with each other is through marriage. With overt, mutual consent, marriage forms a covenant of lifelong companionship between a man and a woman. This commitment is made in the presence of people and accompanied by guidance and advice from a responsible individual.

For this, women, like men, are owners of their will and are completely free to make their decisions within the boundaries set by God. Nothing can be imposed on them without their consent.

Relations Prohibited for Marriage *(Muḥar-ramāt)*

Marriage with one's mother, daughter, sister, aunt or niece is strictly forbidden. God Almighty intends that a mother maintains a purity of regard for her son, a daughter for her father, a sister for her brother, and an aunt for her nephew. These relationships are to remain entirely free from any trace of lust or sexual desire, as such inclinations would undermine human dignity and contradict the inherent sense of modesty that sets humans apart from animals.

The same rule applies to relationships via nursing. Hence, all those relationships which are forbidden by lineage are also forbidden through nursing.

After lineage and nursing, there exists a relationship through marriage. The sanctity of relationships arising from this is evidently clear to human nature. Hence, marriage is forbidden with one's mother-in-law, daughter-in-law, sister-in-law, aunt by marriage, and niece by marriage.

However, since these relationships are established through the intermediary of a wife or husband, they carry a certain vulnerability. Therefore, the Qur'ān has set three specific conditions for them:

1. First, a stepdaughter is only prohibited if the marriage with her mother has been consummated.
2. Second, the prohibition regarding a daughter-in-law applies only if the son is a direct biological descendant.
3. Third, the prohibition concerning a wife's sister, as well as her aunt, niece, and grandniece, applies only while the marital relationship with the wife exists.

Besides these, marriage is also prohibited with a stepmother and a woman already in marriage with another man.

Terms and Conditions

Marriage must include a bridal gift, known as *Mahr*, as a duty ordained by God Almighty, making it a mandatory aspect of the marital contract. The responsibility for providing for the wife and covering household expenses traditionally rests with the man, and the *Mahr* serves as a token of this responsibility.

No specific amount has been prescribed for the *Mahr*; it is left to societal customs and individual discretion. Based on the woman's social status and the man's financial circumstances, they may agree upon any suitable amount.

Chastity is also a condition for marriage. An adulterer may not marry a chaste woman, nor an adulteress a chaste man—unless they have sincerely repented, sought forgiveness for their sin, and the matter of adultery has not been brought before a court.

The same principle applies to polytheism: just as marital unfaithfulness is unacceptable, it is even more intolerable for a Muslim to permit the worship of anyone besides God within their household. In fact, such spiritual disloyalty is graver than physical infidelity.

However, there is an exception regarding Jews and Christians: Muslim men are permitted to marry chaste women from these communities. This is because, although their faiths may contain elements of polytheism, they fundamentally uphold the belief in monotheism.

Rights and Duties

The family unit functions like a small state. Just as every state requires a leader for its formation and stability, the family also necessitates leadership. This role could have been assigned to either men or women.

However, the Qur'ān explains that, based on certain natural abilities, this leadership role has been entrusted to men. Consequently, it expects women, firstly, to adopt an attitude of harmony and cooperation with their husbands, and secondly, to safeguard their husbands' privacy and dignity.

If a woman, in challenging this role of her husband, disrupts the harmony of the household, God has permitted the man to take three steps to preserve the stability of his home:

1. The first step is to advise the wife. The Qur'ān uses the word advice, *(wa'z)* implying that it may involve some level of reproach and censure.

2. The second step is to withdraw from close and informal interactions to signal the seriousness of the matter, helping her understand that a change in behavior is necessary to avoid more severe consequences.

3. The third step is physical discipline, which should be gentle and no more than what a teacher might use with students or a father with his children during training.

These measures should be followed in sequence: the second should be attempted only after the first, and the third only when the husband believes there is no alternative left and all other efforts have proven ineffective. This marks the outer boundary of a husband's disciplinary authority. If this results in reform, no attempts should be made to seek revenge against the woman.

Even if a man dislikes his wife, it is not permissible for a believer to cause her distress, attempt to reclaim what he has given her, or subject her to hardship. Such behavior is justifiable only if she engages in blatant indecency. If she remains loyal, chaste, and modest, then troubling her merely out of personal dislike is unjust and a clear violation of the principles of justice, integrity, and nobility.

Moral corruption is indeed detestable, but a mere lack of attraction or minor disagreements does not justify depriving her of the rights owed to her in a dignified society. Even in times of dissatisfaction, she should be treated with respect—guided by wisdom, compassion, and the enduring principles of mercy, justice, and fairness.

Polygyny

In accordance with the nature upon which humans were

created, the institution of the family—with its fundamental virtues—can only be established through the marriage bond between one man and one woman.

It's the necessities of civilization and the psychological, political, and social benefits which have, more or less, kept the practice of polygyny prevalent in every society, and keeping these in mind, God has not prohibited it in any of His laws.

However, for the welfare of orphans, when the Qur'ān encourages to benefit from this practice, it also imposes two conditions:

1. one is that even for the benefit such as the rights of orphans, the number of women in a man's marriage should not exceed four.

2. The second is that the condition of justice among wives is such an unalterable condition that if a man cannot fulfill it, then even in view of some important religious expediency, it is not lawful for him to contract more than one marriage.

However, this does not mean that there must be no difference in outward behavior and inner affection. Absolute fairness in matters of the heart is beyond human ability, and even with the best of intentions, it cannot be attained. Since a man cannot control the inclinations of his heart, it is sufficient that he does not incline so heavily toward one wife that the other is left neglected or suspended in uncertainty.

Whether the marriage was entered into to safeguard the rights of orphans or for any other reason, bridal gift and fair treatment are the rightful due of the woman and must be given willingly and generously. However, if there is a concern that insisting on full equality among wives might lead the husband to neglect or avoid one of them, then there is no harm if both parties mutually agree to a compromise.

Limits of Sexual Intercourse

Sexual intercourse between husband and wife are prohibited during the periods of menstruation and postnatal bleeding. This restriction remains in effect until the bleeding ceases. However, the proper and recommended course is to resume intimacy only after the woman has attained ritual purity—and even then, in the manner that is permitted and prescribed by God.

Oath of Abstention from Intimacy *(Ilā')*

It is not permissible for a husband to sever intimate relations with his wife without a valid reason. Even if he has taken an oath to do so, the oath must be broken.

A maximum period of four months is prescribed for such a situation. Within this time, the husband must either resume marital relations or, if he chooses not to, proceed with a divorce.

Unlawful Comparison *(Ẓihār)*

If a person arbitrarily says to his wife that she is like his mother or compares any part of her body to any of his mother's parts, it does not make the wife his mother nor can she attain the sanctity of a mother. Therefore, such a comparison does not break the marriage nor does the wife become prohibited for him like a mother.

However, this does not mean that he should be left without any admonition. Such statements have extraordinary effects on the social life of humans; hence it is necessary to discipline him so that he and others may be cautious in the future.

Thus, God decrees that before he can touch his wife, he must pay the expiation for his sin. The expiation is as follows:

- a slave should be freed.
- If that is not possible, then the individual must fast for two consecutive months.
- If even that is not possible, then sixty needy people should be fed.

Divorce

If a husband and wife cannot get along, there has always been provision for separation in the religion of the Prophets. In terminology, this is called divorce.

Before it reaches this point, it should be everyone's desire that the relationship, once established, should be preserved as much as possible from breaking. However, after adopting all possible measures for reform, if the situation does not improve and it becomes clear that the relationship can no longer be maintained, then, as a last resort before divorce, God Almighty has directed the couple's tribe, community, relatives, and well-wishers to step forward and try to mend matters with their influence. It has been prescribed that an arbitrator from the husband's and one from the wife's family be chosen, who together shall endeavor to reconcile them. It is expected that disputes, which the parties themselves could not resolve, may be settled with the intervention of the elders of the family and other well-wishers.

Since the man is the head of the family, and also responsible for providing maintenance and other expenses, the right of divorce has been granted to him. If a woman wants a separation, she will not give the divorce herself, but would demand it from the husband. Under normal circumstances, it is expected that any honorable man, finding no possibility of continuing the marriage, would accept such a demand. However, if this does not happen, the woman can approach a court, which would then order the husband to grant the divorce or decide on the annulment of the marriage.

Whether the husband gives the divorce himself or decides on separation upon the wife's demand, the method prescribed in the Qur'ān is as follows:

1. Divorce shall be given considering the Waiting Period *('idda)*. It implies that it is not permissible to immediately divorce, rather it should be given with the intention to separate after the completion of a specified period. In terminology, *'idda* refers to the period during which a divorced woman or a widow cannot marry another man.

    As this Waiting Period is primarily intended to determine pregnancy status, it is essential that divorce is given after the wife's menstrual period has ended and without any conjugal relations occurring during this time of cleanliness.

2. The Waiting Period must be counted with great care. Divorce is a sensitive matter that affects not only the husband and wife but also their children, families, and numerous legal aspects. It is therefore crucial to note the exact time and date of the divorce, the wife's condition at that moment, the starting point of the Waiting Period, its duration, and the time of its completion.

3. The husband has the right to reconcile at any point

before the Waiting Period concludes. If he does not do so, the marriage will automatically end once the Waiting Period is complete. Therefore, as the end of the period approaches, the husband must decide whether to retain the marital bond or allow it to dissolve. In either case, God commands that the matter be settled in a fair and respectful way.

The directions given in the Qur'ān are as follows:

1. First, any gifts given to the wife—whether property, real estate, jewelry, clothing, or other items—regardless of their value, may not be taken back. Obligatory support (*Nafaqa)* and Bridal Gift *(Mahr)* are her rightful dues, and there is no question of reclaiming them. In fact, the Qur'ān explicitly forbids taking back anything that has been given to the wife. However, there are two exceptions to this rule:

    a. If the couple finds it impossible to live together within the limits set by God—and this is also acknowledged by the community's decision-makers—but the husband refuses to grant a divorce solely to avoid parting with the wealth he has given, then the wife is permitted to return some or all of these assets to obtain her release. In such a case, it is not forbidden for the husband to accept what is returned.

    b. If the wife commits open lewdness. As this fundamentally destroys the basis of the marital relationship, the husband is allowed to take back his given wealth in such cases.

2. Secondly, if divorce takes place before the marriage has been consummated and before the bridal gift *(Mahr)*

has been set, the husband bears no financial obligation. However, if the bridal gift has been stipulated and divorce occurs before consummation, then half of the agreed *Mahr* must be paid—unless the wife willingly waives her right to it, or the husband chooses to pay the full amount.

3. Thirdly, the wife shall be given some means of sustenance upon divorce. The Qur'ān has declared it a right for those who fear God and adopt a kind attitude. Its amount will be determined considering society's norms and the husband's financial status. Even if the divorce is given without consummating the marriage or fixing the bridal gift, God Almighty commands that this right be fulfilled.

4. If the husband reconciles during the Waiting Period, the woman remains his wife. The right to divorce and then reconcile is granted twice within a single marriage. After these two instances, this right no longer remains. Therefore, if the husband divorces his wife a third time after having reconciled with her twice, the separation becomes permanent. She cannot return to him unless she marries another man and that marriage also ends in divorce.

5. Whether the husband divorces or reconciles, he should take two trustworthy Muslims as witnesses to his decision. The purpose is that neither party denies anything later, and if any dispute arises, it can be easily resolved.

6. Generally, the Waiting Period of divorce is three menstrual cycles, and in the case of pregnancy, it lasts until the birth of the child. If the woman has reached menopause or has reached the age of menstruation but has not menstruated, then the Waiting Period will be three

months. For a woman whose marriage has not been consumated, since the question of pregnancy does not arise, there is no Waiting Period for her. The commands related to the period of Waiting Period mentioned in the Qur'ān are as follows:

a. Firstly, it is directed that during this period, neither the wife should leave her home nor does the husband have the right to evict her from the house. Staying together might result in a change of hearts, both might reconsider their behavior, and their broken home may become reestablished once again. The only exception is if the husband has given divorce due to the wife's open lewdness. In such a case, it is not fair to demand that the husband allow such a woman to stay in his house, nor can the benefit intended by this directive be achieved.

b. Secondly, it is stated that during 'idda, the husband will provide her with a living place and maintenance according to his status and will not adopt any method that might hurt her dignity and compel her to leave his house within a few days due to distress.

c. Thirdly, during 'idda, the woman will not attempt to hide her pregnancy. God Almighty has emphasized this strictly because the command of 'idda is given specifically to decide whether the woman is pregnant.

7. Even after divorce, if the father wishes the mother to breastfeed their child, she should do so for up to two years. If she agrees, he must compensate her, and the amount should be determined through mutual consultation in a fair and respectful manner. If the father has passed away,

the same responsibilities and rights are transferred to his heir. Both parties may also agree to a shorter duration. If the father—or his heir—wishes to appoint another woman to breastfeed the child instead, it is permissible, provided all matters agreed upon with the mother have been properly settled.

8. After the divorce, the former husband no longer has any right to interfere in the woman's decisions. She is free to marry whomever she wishes, whenever she chooses. As long as her decision conforms to lawful practice, it cannot be objected to.

Husband's Death

The Waiting Period for a widow is four months and ten days. This duration is longer than that of a divorced woman because, in the case of divorce, it is instructed that it be given during a period of purity in which no intimacy has occurred. Such a condition, however, cannot be applied to a widow. Therefore, from a precautionary standpoint, the Waiting Period was extended. Since the purpose of the Waiting Period is the same for both divorced women and widows, the exceptions outlined for divorce also apply to widows. Accordingly, there is no Waiting Period for a widow whose marriage was not consummated, and the Waiting Period of a pregnant widow ends upon childbirth.

After the Waiting Period is over, the woman is free to take whatever step she deems appropriate in her affairs. However, she should abide by the norms of society, meaning she should not engage in any act that could potentially harm the honor, repute, dignity, and good traditions of families.

With this consideration, no blame is placed on the widow or her guardians. If someone wishes to marry a widow during her

Waiting Period, he may reflect on the matter privately or make a respectful, indirect reference to it—but it is not permissible to disregard the emotions of a grieving family by sending a formal marriage proposal during this time or making a secret commitment..

It is also obligatory for husbands to make a will providing their widows with maintenance and accommodation for one year, unless the widows themselves choose to leave or make alternative arrangements.

Mixed Gatherings

For the protection of the institution of marriage and to maintain the purity of hearts in interpersonal relations, God Almighty has set manners for the mixing of men and women.

These manners are as follows:

1. When there is a need to enter one another's homes, it is not permissible to barge in thoughtlessly and without seeking permission. On such occasions, it is important for a person to introduce himself to the household in a respectful and courteous manner—by offering salutations at the door. This allows the residents to know who is at the door, why he has come, and whether it is appropriate for him to be let in. If they respond to the greeting and grant permission, then he may enter. However, if no one is home or it is made clear that a meeting is not possible at that time, he should leave without taking offense or feeling uneasy.

   This guidance is not meant to deprive friends and family of normal social interaction or to restrict their personal freedoms. Therefore, it is not objectionable for individuals—or their dependent or disabled friends and relatives who live with them—to visit each other's homes, engage in social interaction, and for men and women to dine together or separately, as appropriate.

There is no restriction in their own houses, nor in the houses of their ancestors, mothers, brothers and sisters, uncles, aunts, maternal uncles, and maternal aunts, nor in the houses of those under their guardianship, and neither in friends' houses. However, it is essential to greet and seek permission when entering someone's home.

2. This restriction is not necessary for places where families do not reside such as hotels, inns, guest houses, shops, offices, men's areas, etc. Similarly, servants who frequent homes and underage children are not required to seek permission at every instance.

It suffices for them to seek permission during three times:

- before the Fajr prayer while people are still in their beds;
- at noon when people undress for the midday nap;
- and after the 'Ishā' a prayer when they go to bed.

Apart from these times, underage children and household servants can go to the women and men's private spaces and rooms without seeking permission.

However, this exemption will not remain after they reach puberty. Upon reaching the age of puberty, it will be necessary for them to seek permission according to general law before entering homes.

3. In such gatherings where men and women are present together, God commands both to lower their gazes. This

means exercising modesty and self-restraint in how they look at one another—avoiding lustful stares or excessive attention to physical appearance. The true spirit of this command is not to prohibit all looking or require the gaze to remain permanently lowered, but to prevent inappropriate or prolonged glances.

4. On such occasions, individuals must safeguard their private parts. This means there should be no inappropriate attention directed toward those areas, nor should they be exposed before others. When men and women are present in a same setting, extra care should be taken to ensure proper covering of the private areas.

   A key consideration in such settings is modest dress. Both men and women should wear clothing that adequately covers not only the private parts but also their adornment *(Zīna)* in an appropriate manner. Additionally, care should be taken during gatherings to ensure that one's body remains properly covered while sitting, standing, or moving about.

5. Especially for women, it is important that no item of adornment should be exposed in front of anyone except their close relatives and related persons.

   However, the adornments that are customarily visible are exempt. This includes makeup and ornaments on the hands, feet, and face. Beyond these, women are instructed to conceal their adornments in all other areas. Additionally, they should refrain from striking the ground with their feet in the presence of men to avoid drawing attention to any hidden adornments.

6. Since a woman's chest is also among the private parts, and

there are ornaments around the neck, it is recommended in such instances to cover it with a scarf.

This command to cover the chest and neckline does not apply to elderly women who no longer expect marriage, provided they do not display adornment.

Nonetheless, it is preferred for them too to be cautious and not remove the scarf in the presence of men. This is better for them.

Parents

Among the relationships formed through marriage, the parent–child relationship is one of the most important. Guidance on treating parents with kindness is found in all divine scriptures. The limits set by the Qur'ān for this are as follows:

1. After the Creator, a person should be most grateful to their parents. This gratitude is not just verbal; it necessarily demands that one treats them with utmost respect, does not harbor any resentment towards them in their heart, does not utter disrespectful words in their presence, but rather adopts an approach of gentleness, love, courtesy, and dutiful obedience. One should heed their advice and comfort them in their old age and weakness.

2. Despite the honored status of parents, they do not have the right to compel their children to associate partners with God. In such matters, children must firmly refuse obedience and follow only those who lead them toward God. If parents call them to deviate from God's path, that call must not be accepted. All other divine commands should be understood in this light—it is not permissible

to violate any of them, even at the insistence of one's parents.

3. Even if parents persist in calling their children toward the sin of polytheism, good conduct must still be maintained with them in worldly affairs. Their needs should be met to the best of one's ability, and sincere prayers for their guidance should continue. While matters of faith and law remain separate, the children must not show any negligence in fulfilling their duties toward their parents in these areas.

Orphans

When children lose their father, the Qur'ān provides specific guidance regarding their affairs.

The summary of this guidance is as follows:

1. Guardians must transfer the wealth to orphans when due, refraining from using it for themselves. Consuming an orphan's wealth unjustly is like filling one's belly with fire. Therefore, no one should attempt to substitute their inferior goods for the orphan's better ones, nor should they merge the orphan's property with their own under the pretext of administrative convenience. If a merger occurs, it should solely be for the purpose of safeguarding and better managing the orphan's assets, not for personal gain.

2. Protecting the wealth of orphans and safeguarding their rights is a serious responsibility. If someone finds it difficult to fulfill this duty alone and believes that marrying the orphan's mother would make it easier, they may marry women from among those lawfully permitted—two,

three, or four—provided they are able to uphold justice among them. However, if there is a concern that justice cannot be maintained, then even for a noble cause such as the welfare of orphans, they should marry only one, as this is the best way to uphold justice. Similarly, it is essential that these women are given their bridal gifts justly as other women are. It should not be used as an excuse to claim that, because the marriage was undertaken for the children's welfare, all other responsibilities may be disregarded. However, if they willingly forgive a portion of the bridal gift or grant some other concession, there is no harm in that. People may benefit from it if they so choose.

3. The directive to hand over wealth to orphans should be carried out when they reach an age of maturity and demonstrate the ability to manage it responsibly. Until then, their assets must remain under the supervision and care of their guardians. The guardians should continue to assess whether the orphans are developing the necessary understanding to handle responsibilities. During this period, their needs should be properly fulfilled, and guardians must not misuse or waste their wealth out of fear that the orphans will soon come of age. In all dealings, orphans should be treated with kindness and respect.

4. If the guardians are affluent, they should not take anything in return for their service, but if they are poor, they may take fair compensation from the orphan's wealth, in accordance with customary standards.

5. When handing over wealth, trustworthy and respectable people should be made witnesses to prevent any mistrust or disputes. Then, it should be remembered that one day

this account will also have to be given to God, and He is All-Hearing, All-Knowing; nothing can be hidden from Him.

6. Although the shares of heirs are specified in the deceased's estate, when close relatives, orphans, and the needy are present at the time of distribution, regardless of whether they legally have a right or not, they should be given something and sent off politely. On such occasions, everyone should remember that their children could also become orphans and may face a similar need for compassion from others when they leave this world.

THE LAW OF POLITICS

The innate nature with which God has created humans naturally inclines them toward building civilizations. Sooner or later, to safeguard this civilization from the misuse of free will, humans are compelled to establish systems of societal organization.

Politics and governance arise from this inherent need, as evidenced throughout human history. As long as humanity exists, it cannot escape this necessity, regardless of individual desires. Therefore, rather than dreaming of a society or civilization without governance, it is far more logical to focus on purifying and improving the collective system.

Scholars of divine scriptures understand that there are two regions in the world that Allāh Almighty specifically designated for Himself: Palestine and the Arabian Peninsula. These lands were chosen so that nations selected by Allāh could establish centers of monotheism to bear witness to the truth on a global scale. These centers were established in two mosques located in Mecca and Jerusalem, known as the Kaʿba *(Bayt al-Ḥarām)* and Solomon's Temple *(Haykal Sulaymānī)*. It was ordained that these lands would be safeguarded and that the message of faith would be conveyed to the farthest corners of the world through them, with the condition that followers of any other religion would not be permitted to settle permanently in these regions. Consequently, the governance of these lands was to be entrusted to the nations chosen for this purpose.

The administration of this governance has, at various times in history, been directly under the control of the Almighty Himself. The last occurrence of this was during the Prophethood of Muhammad (PBUH). It was at this moment that a political law for this divine governance was revealed in the Qurʾān, with certain aspects further clarified by God's final Prophet. This is a guiding law aimed at the purification of the collective system and is based on the following five principles:

1. Fundamental Principle

In matters where God and His Messenger have given eternal commands, Muslim authorities—whether heads of state or members of parliament—have no right to legislate on behalf of the people. Therefore, Muslims cannot enact any law in their state that contradicts the commands of God and His Messenger or disregards their guidance. Within this framework, they are nonetheless obligated to give due attention to the directives of their authorities and to abide by them.

2. Fundamental Responsibility

Based on this principle, the primary responsibility of the established collective system is to entrust national duties to individuals according to merit and to strive for the highest standards of justice and fairness in all aspects of life.

3. Religious Duties

Prayer will be established, *Zakāt* will be collected, good will be promoted, and evil will be restrained—these are the religious responsibilities of the state. As outlined in the guidance of the Qur'ān and Sunna, the fulfillment of these duties is to be carried out as follows:

a. Muslim leaders and their representatives will personally observe prayer and ensure that their subordinates are also diligent in performing it.

b. The Friday and *'Īd* prayers, including the sermon and leadership of the prayers, shall be conducted by these leaders or by officials appointed by them in every locality.

c. *Zakāt* is the only tax for Muslims. Therefore, every Muslim on whom *Zakāt* is obligatory must separate the specified portion from their wealth, livestock, and produce, and hand it over to the government. The government, in turn, will strive to meet the needs of its citizens in need, proactively reaching them before they even ask for help.

d. The government will appoint designated officials to promote good and prevent evil, ensuring they work actively within their defined mandates.

5. Rights of Muslims

Muslim citizens who establish prayer and consistently pay *Zakāt* will be entitled to all the rights owed to them as members of the Muslim community within the state. They will be regarded as brothers, equal in legal status. Beyond the affirmative religious obligations—such as prayer and *Zakāt*—no other element of faith shall be enforced by law. Furthermore, the state has no authority to infringe upon their life, property, honor, intellect, or freedom of opinion.

6. System of Governance

The selection of state leaders and officials, as well as the formation of the government, will be carried out through public consultation and the opinion of the people. Even after assuming office, those in leadership will not have the authority to disregard the consensus or majority opinion of the Muslim community in collective affairs.

THE ECONOMIC LAW

The law for the purification of the economy that Allāh has given to humanity through His final Prophet is founded on the principle that this world has been created as a place of trial. For this reason, Allāh has established its system in such a way that every human being is both dependent on others and serves as a support for others. In this world, even the most exalted individuals are in need of others to fulfill their requirements, and at times, they must turn to even the most ordinary people to meet those needs.

Every individual has a role, and no one can live entirely independently. The Creator has endowed people with varying levels of intelligence, skills, preferences, and resources. Due to this diversity, we find scholars and sages whose wisdom illuminates the world; writers whose words give lasting life to ideas; researchers whose groundbreaking discoveries are celebrated through generations; leaders whose strategies shape the complexities of social life; reformers who awaken humanity to self-awareness; and rulers whose resolve shapes the course of history.

On the other hand, there are laborers, farmers, servants, porters, and cleaners whose hard work creates wonders: they turn soil into wealth, produce delights for the palate, make homes shine, pave paths ready to be traveled, raise buildings that reach the sky, and clear away filth before the first light of day.

By creating the world with these different ranks, the Lord observes whether people of higher and lower status build a righteous society and civilization through mutual respect and cooperation, or whether they fall into conflict and harm one another, turning the world into chaos and thus bringing disgrace upon themselves in this life and deserving punishment in the hereafter.

This is the trial of humanity, in which God Almighty has provided guidance through His Prophets regarding economic activity and has given a law for its purification and refinement. This law is as follows:

1. Illegitimate Consumption of Other's Wealth

It is prohibited to acquire or consume others' wealth through unjust or illegitimate means *(akl al-amwāl bi'l-bāṭil)*. Usury and gambling are among the gravest offenses in this category. Beyond these, the le-gitimacy of all other economic transactions should also be evaluated based on this principle.

2. Public Properties

All wealth and property that is not privately owned or cannot be attributed to an individual should remain under state ownership. This ensures that national resources do not circulate exclusively among the wealthy, allowing the underprivileged to benefit as well. Moreover, such assets can be used to support various responsibilities associated with the collective system.

3. Documentation and Testimony

For lending, loans, wills, and other financial matters, documentation and arranging for testimony are essential. Neglect in this matter sometimes leads to significant ethical corruption.

The directives are as follows:

- If the transaction of the loan is for a specific period, it is imperative to document it.

- This document should be written by a scribe in the presence of both parties, justly.

- The borrower is responsible for having the document prepared. The document should state: "I am indebted to the son of so-and-so in the amount of...".

- If the person is of limited understanding, elderly, or unable to write, then his guardian or representative should have the document prepared truthfully and justly.

- The testimony should be recorded by two Muslim men who are reliable, credible, trustworthy, and known for good character and conduct.

- If two men possessing the aforementioned qualities are not available, then one man and two women can be chosen. The reason for requiring two women is so that if one woman feels overwhelmed or confused in the court's environment, the other can support her to prevent the testimony from being clouded by confusion or doubt.

- Those who have been part of the testimony as witnesses should not refuse to testify when called upon.

- Casual transactions do not mandate documentation and testimony. However, for significant purchases or sales, witnesses should be appointed to settle any disputes that may arise.

- In case of disputes, neither the scribe nor witnesses should be harmed by any party.

- If someone is on a journey and unable to find a scribe, the transaction may proceed by offering collateral. This collateral is permissible only until the lender is assured of repayment. Once that assurance is established, the collateral must be returned.

- If someone is approaching death and wishes to make a will regarding their property, they should appoint two trustworthy individuals from among their fellow Muslims to witness it.

- If someone faces death while on a journey and cannot find two Muslim witnesses, they may appoint two non-Muslims as witnesses out of necessity.

- If there is concern that the appointed Muslim witnesses might alter their testimony in favor of someone, to prevent this, an arrangement can be made for them to swear by God, after a prayer in the mosque, that they will not alter their testimony for personal gain or favoritism, even if the beneficiary is a close relative. They should be reminded that any deviation will render them sinners.

- Witnesses must realize that their testimony is indeed a testimony before God; therefore, even the slightest act of treachery on their part not only makes them betrayers of people but also of God.

- Nonetheless, if it is later discovered that the witnesses have shown favoritism or acted unjustly against the testator's will, then two individuals from among those whose rights were infringed may stand and declare under oath that their testimony is more truthful than that of the original witnesses. They will affirm that they have not strayed from the truth in this matter and solemnly assert that if they do so, they will be deemed unjust before God.

- The benefit of this added layer of accountability for witnesses is that it encourages them to provide truthful testimony. Otherwise, they risk having their oaths nullified by the counter-oaths of others, leading to their testimony being rejected despite being the primary witnesses.

4. Distribution of Inheritance

After a Muslim passes away, their wealth must necessarily be distributed among their heirs in the following manner:

a. Firstly, if there are any debts owed by the deceased, these are to be paid from the estate. Then, if a will has been made, it should be executed. After this, the inheritance will be divided.

b. An heir cannot be given more than their legal share through a will, unless exceptional circumstances—such as their service, need, or specific situation—justify it.

c. After allocating shares to the parents and the spouse, the remaining estate belongs to the deceased's children.

d. If the deceased leaves behind no sons but two or more daughters, they will receive two-thirds of the remaining estate.

e. If there is only one daughter, she is entitled to half.

f. If the deceased leaves behind only sons, the entire estate will be divided among them.

g. If there are both sons and daughters, a son's share will be equivalent to that of two daughters, and the entire estate will be divided among them in this manner.

h. In the absence of children, the deceased's siblings act as substitutes. After allocating shares to parents and spouse(s), these siblings become the heirs.

i. If both parents are alive and the deceased has children or siblings, each parent receives one-sixth of the estate. If there are no children or siblings, and only the parents are the heirs, then one-third of the estate goes to the mother and two-thirds to the father.

j. If the deceased is a man with children, his wife will receive one-eighth of the estate. If there are no children, the wife is entitled to one-fourth.

k. If the deceased is a woman without children, half of the estate goes to her husband, but if she has children, the husband receives a quarter.

1. If none of the primary heirs are present, the deceased may designate someone to inherit. If the designated heir is a relative who has only one brother or sister, that sibling receives one-sixth of the estate, and the remaining five-sixths go to the designated heir. If the relative has more than one sibling, they together receive one-third of the estate, and the remaining two-thirds go to the designated heir.

This distribution is based on beneficial kinship, with differences in shares reflecting the varying degrees of benefit the heirs provided to the deceased. Since a daughter's benefit typically transfers to her husband after marriage, and likewise, a husband provides both companionship and financial support to his wife, sons receive twice the share of daughters, and husbands receive twice the share of wives.

THE LAW OF CALLING TO FAITH *(DAʿWA)*

A fundamental requirement of religion is that those who embrace the truth in this world must, after accepting it, continually encourage and share it with others. This duty is generally known as invitation *(Daʿwa)* and propagation *(Tablīgh).*

The Qurʾān establishes that the responsibility of invitation rests on believers in various capacities, each with its own distinct approach.

We can discuss this under the following headings:

The Invitation of Prophets

All Prophets sent by God were tasked with calling people to Him *(Daʿwa ilā Allāh)* and delivering both warnings and glad tidings. While the role of issuing warnings and conveying glad tidings is common to all Prophets and requires no explanation, however, among those prophets entrusted with the role of messengership, the Qur'ān states that they were commanded to deliver warnings to their people in such a way that it stands as a testimony *(Shahāda)* for or against them.

In Quranic terminology, Testimony refers to presenting the truth with such clarity that no excuse for denial or deviation remains. To fulfill this purpose, God appoints His Messengers not only to convey His message but also to establish His religion and, through them and their followers, enact a minor Day of Reckoning on earth—an example of divine judgment before the final Day of Judgment. They are clearly informed that if they remain faithful to their covenant with God, they will be rewarded; if they deviate, they will be punished in this very life. Their lives thus become a visible sign of divine authority, embodying God's justice on earth.

Furthermore, these Messengers are commanded to convey the truth they have witnessed with absolute clarity and unwavering conviction. This is what constitutes the Testimony *(Shahāda)*. The invitation of the Messengers, after progressing through successive phases—beginning with a focused call, then a public proclamation, followed by Conclusive Establishment of Truth and culminating in separation and disassociation—becomes the very basis for divine judgment, both in this world and in the Hereafter.

Thus, God grants ascendancy to these Messengers and brings His divine punishment upon those who reject their message—within this very world.

The Invitation of the Progeny of Abraham (PBUH)

This invitation is the same Testimony *(Shahāda)* mentioned above. The Qurʾān has informed us that the progeny of Abraham (PBUH) was also selected by God Almighty for this Testimony and commanded to strive to fulfill its requirements, just as He selects certain noble beings from among the children of Adam (PBUH) for Prophethood and Messengership.

If the descendants of Abraham (PBUH) remain steadfast in the truth and convey it to all nations with clarity and conviction, God Almighty grants them dominion over those nations that reject their message. However, if they deviate from this path, He brings upon them humiliation and subjugation at the hands of those very nations.

The Invitation of the Scholars

After the Prophet Muhammad (PBUH), the responsibility of conveying warnings has been transferred to the scholars of this Umma. God Almighty has commanded that from every community of Muslims, some individuals should step forward, acquire religious knowledge, and serve as warners to guide their people and help save them from the torment of the Hereafter.

The Qurʾān highlights certain essential principles for this type of invitation:

1. **Conviction in Truth:** Those who take on this mission must have unwavering faith in the truth they convey. Their hearts and minds should be fully convinced of it, feeling it as the very echo of their hearts and the cry of their souls. They must enter this field with total surrender to their Lord, being the first to wholeheartedly embrace and believe in what they invite others to accept.

2. **Consistency Between Words and Deed:** There must be no contradiction between their words and actions. They should proclaim and embody the principles they stand for, allowing their actions to testify to the truth they present to others.

3. **Uncompromising Truthfulness:** They must not compromise on the truth. Every truth that becomes evident to them—no matter how small—should be acknowledged, testified to openly, and conveyed to the world without concern for criticism.

4. **Use of the Qur'ān as a Warning:** The Qur'ān must serve as their primary means of delivering warnings, as the Prophet Muhammad (PBUH) was commanded by the Qur'ān to do so. It is on this basis that he was appointed as a warner for the entire world. Scholars, in reality, convey this warning to the people on behalf of the Prophet.

The Invitation of the State

When Muslims attain political sovereignty in a land, it becomes their duty to appoint individuals from within their community to promote virtue, prevent wrongdoing, and advocate for righteousness. Once a government is established, this responsibility rests with the decision-makers of the Muslim community. They must fulfill this obligation alongside addressing the other inherent responsibilities of governance.

The Invitation of the Individual

The individual's role involves advising others within their sphere of influence to promote virtue and prevent wrongdoing. In this form of invitation, the roles of inviter and invitee are closely intertwined—each person is both inviting others and being invited at all times.

This responsibility applies to all relationships: a father to his son and a son to his father, a wife to her husband and a husband to his wife, a brother to his sister and a sister to her brother, a friend to a friend, and a neighbor to a neighbor. In essence, each person must fulfill this duty toward everyone they are connected with. Whenever one notices that someone in their circle has deviated from the path of truth, they should guide them toward righteousness to the best of their knowledge and ability.

It is possible that we may encourage someone to do good in the morning, and by evening, they may do the same for us. Today, we may fulfill someone's right, and tomorrow, they may remind us of ours. The point is that whenever the opportunity arises, every Muslim must consistently carry out this responsibility within their own sphere of influence.

The Strategy of Invitation

This strategy applies to all forms of invitation. The Qurʾān presents it as a foundational principle based on the following three key points:

1. The invitation must always be conveyed with wisdom, uplifting exhortation, and the most refined argumentation. Wisdom entails presenting logical evidence and sound reasoning, while uplifting exhortation emphasizes compassionate reminders and guidance. The key is that the inviter's words should be rooted in evidence, knowledge, and intellect, delivered in a manner that draws attention through kindness, compassion, and love, rather than through intimidation or dominance. Even during debates or arguments, the inviter should employ respectful and

constructive methods. If the opponent resorts to provocation, the inviter must maintain civility and courtesy, refraining from responding in a similar manner.

2. The inviter's responsibility is solely to extend the invitation. This involves conveying the message clearly, explaining the truth from all angles, and making every effort to encourage and guide. Once this duty has been fulfilled, their responsibility ends. The guidance or misguidance of individuals lies entirely in the hands of God, who knows best who deviates from His path and who remains guided. Consequently, each will be dealt with according to what they deserve. The inviter should neither act as an enforcer nor assume the role of judging others' ultimate fate, such as assigning them to heaven or hell. These matters are exclusively within God's domain. The inviter's duty is solely to convey the message—and they must never, ever exceed this role.

3. If those addressed by the invitation resort to oppression, hostility, or harassment, the inviter can seek retribution within ethical limits, proportional to the harm suffered. However, God encourages patience as the higher path. This patience involves enduring hardships without seeking revenge, remaining steadfast despite trials and difficulties, and refusing to compromise or alter the truth. Those who exhibit such patience are promised a great reward. In time, the fruits of their perseverance will appear in the best form in this world, and by God's will, they will experience even greater outcomes in the Hereafter.

THE LAW OF *JIHĀD*

Peace and liberty are fundamental pillars of human civilization. While individual acts of rebellion are addressed through correction and punishment, when
entire nations become rebellious, it is widely recognized that
there may be no option but to take up arms against them.

As long as guidance and counsel remain effective, resorting
to force is neither necessary nor justifiable. However, when a
nation's defiance escalates to the point where they cannot be
redirected toward the right path through advice and persuasion,
it becomes a collective responsibility to take action. In such
cases, the use of force is warranted to restore a state of peace
and freedom in the world.

The Qur'ān emphasizes that had this permission not been
granted, the rebellion of nations would have escalated to such
an extent that it would have led to the complete destruction of

civilization. Places of worship—where the name of God, the Lord of the Worlds, is invoked, and worship is carried out day and night—would have been reduced to ruins, abandoned, left to gather dust.

In Islamic law, *Jihād*[7] is undertaken with this specific and noble purpose. It is not waged to satisfy personal desires, acquire wealth, expand territories, establish governance, gain fame, or achieve glory. Nor is it driven by pride, tribalism, enmity, or any other form of self-interest. This form of *Jihād* is entirely free from human selfishness or personal motives. It is a divine undertaking—a battle fought for God, by His servants, under His command, and in accordance with His guidance. Those who participate in this effort do so as instruments of God's will, serving solely to fulfill His objectives. They have no personal agenda or interests in this endeavor and cannot deviate from their assigned role in any way.

This law states:

1. The Command of *Jihād*

The command of *Jihād* and combat in Islam was given to Muslims as a community, not as individuals. In the Qur'ānic verses revealed on this subject, Muslims are not addressed in their individual capacity at all. Similar to the implementation of the Islamic Penal System *(Ḥudūd and Ta'zīrāt)*, these instructions are directed at the community as a whole. Consequently, the authority to take action in matters of *Jihād* rests solely with the collective body. No individual or group within the community has

---

7. Jihad means to exert one's full effort in a struggle. In the Qur'ān, this term is used both for general striving in the path of God and specifically for armed struggle in God's cause *(qital fi sabi-lillah)*. In this context, it refers to the latter meaning.

the right to independently make decisions or act on their behalf in this regard.

2. The Purpose of *Jihād*

In the Qurʾān, the command of *Jihād* was primarily issued to eliminate *Fitna*, which refers to forcing individuals to renounce their faith through oppression or coercion. In English, this is commonly described as *persecution*. Additionally, other forms of aggression—whether against life, property, freedom of thought, or expression—are also included within this broader concept. Hence, it can be undertaken against all forms of oppression and aggression.

3. The Obligation of *Jihād*

Jihād does not become obligatory for Muslims until their military strength reaches a certain threshold against the enemy. Therefore, it is essential that to fulfill the responsibility of *Jihād* and combat, they not only maintain their moral integrity but also enhance their military capabilities to the level that the Qurʾān commanded the Muslims at the time of the Prophet, establishing a ratio of one to two between the Muslims and their adversaries, taking into account the circumstances of that era.

4. Participation in *Jihād*

Failing to participate actively in *Jihād* is considered a crime only when a Muslim refrains from joining despite a general call to arms. In such a situation, this neglect becomes a grave sin, comparable to hypocrisy. Outside of this context, however, *Jihād* is regarded as a virtue that every individual should strive to achieve. It is a commendable act, but not an obligatory duty whose neglect would make one culpable.

5. Fleeing from *Jihād*

Showing cowardice and fleeing from the battlefield after engaging in *Jihād* and combat is forbidden. A person of faith should never commit such an act. It is a crime of losing trust in God's support, prioritizing the worldly life over the hereafter, and considering one's life and death are determined solely by personal strategy, which cannot be reconciled with faith.

6. Moral Boundaries

Jihād cannot be conducted disregarding moral constraints. Morality is paramount in all conditions and over everything, and even on the occasion of war, God has not permitted anyone to deviate from moral principles. The most important guidance mentioned in the Qur'ān under this command is the observance of treaties.

Betrayal and breaking of treaties are considered the worst of sins by God. Hence, even if a treaty-bound nation oppresses Muslims, it is not permissible to aid them by violating the treaty. Likewise, action against those who wish to remain neutral during war is not allowed.

When engaging in *Jihād*, a believer must also refrain from arrogance or any display of ostentation. Demonstrations of grandeur or extravagance are unbecoming of a person of faith. In both moments of struggle and celebration, humility and the modesty of servitude should always be prominent.

7. Divine Support

Muslims fight these battles relying on God, but the Qur'ān has made it clear that patience and perseverance are the primary means of obtaining God's support. A group of Muslims does not become entitled to divine support until they develop this quality within themselves.

8. Prisoners of War

Muslims can either release prisoners of war or take ransom from them, but the Qur'ān has forever closed the door on killing them or keeping them as slaves and concubines.

9. Spoils of War

The spoils of war are primarily designated for collective benefit. God has not granted the warriors in God's cause *(Mujāhidīn)* an absolute or permanent right over them, nor is the Muslim government obligated to distribute them in every situation. Rather, it is given the discretion to manage and allocate these spoils in a way that best serves the prevailing circumstances and the broader needs of society and civilization.

FIXED & DISCRETION-ARY PUNISHMENTS

The gift of free will and choice is the greatest honor bestowed upon humans in this world. However, when misused, it inevitably leads to corruption on Earth. This corruption was first manifested through Cain (Qābil), the son of Adam (PBUH), emphasizing the need for measures to safeguard humanity from its own evils and destructive tendencies.

The primary objective in such matters is the eradication of evil and corruption, which must always remain the focus. However, those who have accepted God's guidance and believed in His Messengers are not to be treated as ordinary criminals. The Qur'ān makes it clear that if such individuals commit grave offenses against life, property, or societal order, it is God's decree that they be punished in this world. This punishment serves as a warning to others, reminding them of the punishment of the Hereafter through the demonstration of divine retribution in this life. Moreover, for the offenders themselves, this punishment can serve as a means of purification from their sins if they sincerely choose the path of repentance and reform.

The punishments in such cases have always been severe, serving a dual purpose: to eliminate the crime and to subject the culprits to divine retribution while deterring others. These individuals had knowingly submitted themselves to God and His Messengers, pledged their allegiance to Him, embraced His religion, and yet committed offenses of such gravity that their guilt was ultimately exposed, leading the matter to the courts.

These crimes include:

1. Insurrection and spreading corruption on Earth
2. Homicide and assault
3. Adultery and fornication
4. False Accusation of Adultery
5. Theft.

The punishments for only these crimes are explicitly specified in *Sharīʿah*. For their lesser forms and other crimes beyond these, God has entrusted the matter to the decision-makers of the Muslim community, empowering them to establish appropriate laws and penalties through mutual consultation.

However, it is firmly established that, according to the Qurʾān, the death penalty can only be administered for two offenses: Murder and Spreading corruption on earth *(Fasād fī al-arḍ)*. Moreover, the responsibility to enforce these punishments is entrusted to the entire Muslim community—not to individuals—and is carried out through their collective legal and judicial system.

Here we will clarify these punishments:

Insurrection and Corruption on Earth

If the Messenger of God is present in the world and individuals rebel against any of his orders or decisions under his governance, such rebellion is regarded as defiance against God and His Messenger *(Muḥāraba)*. This defiance is also classified as causing corruption on Earth *(fasād fī al-arḍ)*, particularly when an individual or group challenges the law by engaging in acts that threaten lives, property, honor, and the collective will of the people.

Therefore, when murder takes the form of terrorism, fornication becomes rape and theft assumes the shape of robbery or, pursuing debauchery as a profession, openly indulging in libertine behavior, engaging in hooliganism, sexual deviance threatening the honor of respectable individuals, rebelling against the state's authority, or committing serious crimes such as kidnapping, sabotage, intimidation, and other activities that undermine peace and security are classified as acts of corruption on earth.

The perpetrators will be deemed criminals of causing corruption on Earth.

Four punishments have been prescribed for their suppression:

1. Execution in a manner that serves as a deterrent.

2. Crucifixion in a deterrent-inducing manner.

3. Amputation of limbs from opposite sides.

4. Exile from the land.

Regarding these punishments, certain points have been mentioned as guidelines and conditions:

1. The Qur'ān has given the government the authority to decide which of these punishments is appropriate based on the nature of the crime, the circumstances of the criminal, and the current and expected consequences of the crime. Among these severe punishments, the inclusion of exile as a punishment allows for leniency if circumstances call for it.

2. If the crime is committed by a gang or criminal group, the punishment will apply to all its members rather than only to the individual who carried out a specific act. Therefore, if such a group engages in acts of corruption on Earth—such as murder, rape, kidnapping, sabotage, intimidation, or similar offenses—it is not necessary to identify precisely which individuals committed each act. Every member of the gang will share responsibility for the crime and will be held accountable accordingly.

3. No sympathy should be harbored for such criminals when administering their punishments. Their Creator, the Lord of all, has decreed that they deserve complete disgrace in this world as a consequence of their heinous crimes. This fundamental purpose of these punishments must always be upheld and remembered.

4. If such criminals voluntarily surrender before any government action is initiated against them, they will be treated as ordinary offenders rather than as those accused of rebellion or corruption on Earth.

Retaliation for Homicide and Assault

Retribution *(Qiṣāṣ)* is a divine obligation placed upon the collective Muslim community by God Almighty. It serves as a means to preserve life within society and is a divine law from which only those who act unjustly deviate. It is, therefore, the duty of the government to identify and apprehend murderers within its jurisdiction and to implement *Qiṣāṣ* in accordance with the prescribed law.

In enforcing retribution, equality must be upheld: if the offender is a slave, the retaliation must also involve the same slave; if the offender is a free person, then the same free person shall be subject to punishment. A person's societal or social status should not influence this matter at all. If the victims or the heirs of the murdered or injured decide not to seek life for life, limb for limb, wound for wound, and are willing to show leniency towards the criminal, the court may impose a lesser punishment considering the nature of the crime and the circumstances of the criminal. This is a concession and favor from God to the people. If the victims adopt this, their forgiveness will serve as an expiation for their sins before God Almighty.

In such cases, blood money *(Diya)* must be paid by the offender. God Almighty has commanded that this compensation be determined and distributed in accordance with the community's customs, ensuring utmost fairness.

If the death is accidental and the victim is a Muslim citizen of the offender's country or a member of a treaty nation, the offender is obligated to pay blood money in accordance with societal laws, unless forgiveness is granted. Additionally, as an act of atonement and repentance before God, the offender must free a Muslim slave. However, if the victim is a Muslim from an enemy nation, the offender is not obligated to pay blood money. In such cases, freeing a Muslim slave alone suffices as expiation for the sin. If a slave is unavailable in either scenario, the offender must instead fast for two consecutive months as a means of repentance and purification.

Adultery

For those found guilty of adultery, whether male or female, the prescribed punishment is one hundred lashes if the crime is conclusively proven. This punishment is to be carried out in the presence of a group of Muslims, serving both as a public disgrace for the offender and as a deterrent to others. The Qurʾān explicitly commands that no government or court of believers should show leniency in enforcing this penalty.

Following this punishment, it is prohibited for any chaste man or woman to marry the adulterer or adulteress, as this has been explicitly forbidden by God Almighty.

This is the maximum punishment for this crime and is reserved exclusively for those who have committed it in its most complete and final form, and who, based on their circumstances, are not deemed deserving of leniency. Consequently, individuals who are unable to endure the punishment due to physical or mental incapacity, those coerced into committing the crime, or those lacking the environment, circumstances, or protective measures necessary to avoid such actions are exempt from this penalty.

False Accusation of Adultery

There are two possible scenarios:

1. One is when a person accuses an honorable and virtuous woman or man of adultery.

2. The second is when such a situation arises between a husband and wife.

In the first case, the person must present four eyewitnesses under all circumstances. If he fails to do so, he will be deemed guilty of false accusation, the punishment for which is that he will be flogged with eighty lashes, and his testimony will not be accepted in any matter henceforth. The Qur'ān declares that those who commit this crime will be regarded as transgressors in the sight of God Almighty, unless they sincerely repent for their actions and amend their future behavior.

In the second scenario, if no testimony is available, the matter will be resolved through oaths. The husband must swear by God four times that his accusation is truthful, and on the fifth oath, he must invoke God's curse upon himself if he is lying. If the wife does not defend herself with a similar oath, she will face the prescribed punishment for adultery according to *Sharī'ah*.

However, if the wife denies the accusations, she can exonerate herself by swearing by God four times that her husband is lying, and on the fifth oath, invoking the wrath of God upon herself if he is truthful.

The same procedure applies if a wife accuses her husband of adultery.

Theft

The punishment for theft is the amputation of the hand. Regardless of whether the thief is a man or a woman, if the crime is conclusively proven, the offender's right hand will be amputated from the wrist as a penalty. Similar to the punishment for adultery, this is the maximum penalty for this crime and is only administered when the offender, based on the nature of the crime and their circumstances, is deemed ineligible for any leniency.

DIETARY GUIDELINES

Religion seeks to purify every aspect of human life. Along with the purification of the inner self, it emphasizes on the importance of distinguishing between pure and impure items in food and drink.

Human nature generally offers clear guidance on this matter, allowing people to instinctively differentiate between what is pure and impure for consumption. Throughout history, humans have recognized that animals like lions, leopards, eagles, crows, vultures, snakes, scorpions, and even humans themselves are not suitable for eating. Similarly, they understand that animals such as elephants, horses, and donkeys are not intended for consumption but are instead meant for tasks like riding and utility.

They are also well aware of the impurity of these animals' feces and urine. Similarly, their intellect typically leads them to the correct understanding of the harmfulness and filthiness of intoxicating substances. For this reason, God's law has largely entrusted this matter to human nature itself.

Occasionally, human nature may deviate or become corrupted; however, an examination of global dietary practices reveals that the vast majority of people generally make correct distinctions in this matter.

As a result, the *Sharī'ah* does not extensively regulate this area. Instead, it focuses on specific cases involving animals and their by-products where human reasoning and natural instincts alone are insufficient to determine their permissibility or prohibition.

The pig, while categorized as livestock, also consumes meat like predatory animals, raising the question of whether it should be regarded as edible. Similarly, for animals that are typically slaughtered for consumption, what is their status if they die without being slaughtered according to Islamic rites? Should their blood be deemed as impure as their feces and urine, or can it be considered permissible and pure? Additionally, if an animal is slaughtered in the name of anyone other than God, does it remain lawful for consumption?

As it was challenging for humans to provide clear and definitive answers to these questions, God Almighty, through His Prophets, revealed that pigs, blood, carrion, and animals slaughtered in the name of anyone other than God are impure and must be avoided for consumption.

The explanations given in the Qur'ān regarding this injunction are as follows:

1. Animals that die naturally or perish in sudden accidents are regarded as carrion. Likewise, an animal that has

been mauled by a predator is also considered carrion unless it is slaughtered while still alive.

2. If a trained hunting animal kills prey and the prey dies before it can be slaughtered, the act of killing by the trained animal is regarded as its slaughter, making the prey permissible to eat without further slaughtering. However, this is only valid if the hunting animal has captured the prey for its owner without consuming any part of it. If the animal has eaten from the prey, the catch becomes unlawful.

3. An animal also becomes unlawful if it is sacrificed at a shrine. Similarly, even if the slaughter was not dedicated to anyone other than God, but God's name was also not recited over it, it still falls under this prohibition. This also applies to a hunted animal or any slaughtered animal where God's name was pronounced by someone who either does not believe in God or believes in Him merely as one among other deities, and regards polytheism, in principle, as his religion.

4. The only exception to these prohibitions is in a state of dire necessity, and even then, only to the extent that the person is neither desiring it nor exceeding the limit of necessity.

CUSTOMS AND ETIQUETTE

The manners of living and the cultural expressions that signify a person's refinement and character are collectively referred to as customs and etiquette.

Throughout history, no human society has been without customs and etiquette. They have been consistently observed across all tribes, nations, and civilizations, serving as a shared standard of behavior and conduct.

The identity of nations and communities is largely shaped by these customs and etiquette. Even the Prophets, peace be upon them, who brought divine guidance, emphasized the importance of adhering to specific customs and etiquette.

Since the ultimate aim of religion is the purification of the self, the customs and etiquette prescribed by religion are designed to serve this purpose.

These customs and etiquette include:

1. Mentioning the name of God before eating and drinking with the right hand. The former is for acknowledging and expressing gratitude for the blessings of God Almighty and to pray for their increase, and the latter serves as a constant reminder that on the Day of Judgement, those who will be granted the blessings of Paradise will receive their record of deeds in their right hands.

2. Greeting with *"Peace be upon you"* (al-salāmu ʿalaykum) and its response upon meeting.

3. Saying *"All praise is to God"* (al-hamdu li-llāh) when sneezing and responding with *"May God have mercy on you"* (yarḥamuka Allāh).

4. Keeping the mustache trimmed.

5. Removing the pubic hair.

6. Removing the armpit hairs.

7. Clipping nails.

8. Circumcising boys.

9. Cleaning the nose, mouth, and teeth.

10. Washing private parts after relieving oneself *(Istinjāʾ)*.

11. The ritual bath following menstruation and postnatal bleeding.

12. The ritual bath after sexual impurity *(Ghusl al-janāba)*.

13. Washing, shrouding, and burying the deceased.

14. Celebrating the festivals of ʿĪd al-Fiṭr and ʿĪd al-ʾAḍḥā.

OATH AND EXPIATION OF OATH

I
n religion, the importance of an oath holds exceptional significance. Keeping promises is one of the fundamental ethical principles in Islam, and an oath elevates a pledge to its highest level of seriousness. When a Muslim swears by God regarding a decision, intention, or commitment, they essentially call upon their Lord, the Creator and Sovereign of the universe, as a witness to their words.

Despite the importance of oaths, there are situations where fulfilling an oath becomes impractical or where doing so would lead to a violation of rights—whether God's, one's own, or others'. In such cases, breaking the oath is not only allowed but may, in certain circumstances, become a religious and ethical necessity. To address this, *Sharīʿah* provides a prescribed method for expiation.

The ruling is as follows:

1. Sometimes, an oath is entirely trivial, meaningless, or insignificant. While believers are advised to avoid making such oaths, it is a great mercy from God Almighty that He does not hold individuals accountable for such oaths, either in this world or in the hereafter.

2. To the contrary, if an oath is undertaken with firm resolve and intent—such as forming a binding agreement, affecting rights and obligations, or influencing matters related to what God has permitted or prohibited—then one will certainly be held accountable by God Almighty. Therefore, oaths should never be taken lightly or whimsically, but safeguarded with the utmost responsibility and seriousness.

3. If breaking such an oath becomes necessary for any reason, it is obligatory to offer expiation. The prescribed method of expiation includes feeding ten poor individuals to the standard one normally provides for their family, clothing them, or freeing a slave. If none of these options are possible, fasting for three consecutive days is required.